Dorothy Baker.

84 Southmoor Rd.

Oxford

Nov. 4th 1919.

THE OPEN ROAD

OTHER WORKS BY E. V. LUCAS

THE OPEN ROAD

A Little Book for Wayfarers

COMPILED BY

E. V. LUCAS

"Life is sweet, brother. . . . There's day and
night, brother, both sweet things; sun, moon, and
stars, all sweet things; there's likewise a wind on
the heath."—*Lavengro*

METHUEN & CO. LTD.

36 ESSEX STREET W.C.

LONDON

Twenty-Seventh Edition

Originally Published by Mr. Grant Richards   April 1899
Reprinted November 1899, September 1900, August 1901
*   November 1902, June 1904*
First Published (Seventh Edition, Fcap. 8vo),
*   by Methuen & Co. . . . . November 1905*
Eighth Edition 1905
Ninth and Tenth Editions 1906
Eleventh and Twelfth Editions 1907
Thirteenth and Fourteenth Editions 1908
Fifteenth Edition 1909
Sixteenth and Seventeenth Editions 1910
Eighteenth Edition 1911
Nineteenth Edition 1912
First Published (Twentieth Edition,
*   Crown 4to) . . . . September 1913*
Twenty-first and Twenty-second Editions (Fcap. 8vo) 1913
Twenty-Third Edition (Crown 4to) 1914
Twenty-fourth Edition (Fcap. 8vo) 1914
Twenty-fifth Edition (Fcap. 8vo) 1916
Twenty-sixth Edition (Fcap. 8vo) 1917
Twenty-seventh Edition (Fcap. 8vo) 1918

The End Papers are from designs by William Hyde

TO B.

Alone, the country life—how sweet !
*   But wood and meadow, heath and hill,*
The dewy morn, the noonday heat,
The nest half-hid, the poppied wheat,
*   The peaty purling rill,*
The brake fern's odorous retreat,
The hush of eve, serene, discreet—
*   With you are sweeter still.*

And this shall be for music when no one else is near,
The fine song for singing, the rare song to hear !
That only I remember, that only you admire,
Of the broad road that stretches, and the roadside fire.

R. L. Stevenson.

ARGUMENT

THIS little book aims at nothing but providing companionship on the road for city-dwellers who make holiday. It has no claims to completeness of any kind : it is just a garland of good or enkindling poetry and prose fitted to urge folk into the open air, and, once there, to keep them glad they came—to slip easily from the pocket beneath a tree or among the heather, and provide lazy reading for the time of rest, with perhaps a phrase or two for the feet to step to and the mind to brood on when the rest is over.

E. V. L.

April 1899.

And hark ! how blithe the Throstle sings !
  He, too, is no mean preacher :
Come forth into the light of things,
  Let Nature be your teacher.

She has a world of ready wealth,
  Our minds and hearts to bless—
Spontaneous wisdom breathed by health,
  Truth breathed by cheerfulness.

One impulse from a vernal wood
  May teach you more of man,
Of moral evil and of good,
  Than all the sages can.

Sweet is the lore which Nature brings ;
  Our meddling intellect
Misshapes the beauteous form of things ;
  We murder to dissect.

Enough of Science and of Art ;
  Close up these barren leaves ;
Come forth, and bring with you a heart
  That watches and receives.

William Wordsworth.

TABLE OF CONTENTS

FAREWELL TO WINTER AND THE TOWN

THE ROAD

SPRING AND THE BEAUTY OF THE EARTH

xii

SUN AND CLOUD, AND THE WINDY HILLS

COMPANIONS

BIRDS, BLOSSOMS, AND TREES

SUMMER SPORTS AND PASTIMES

REFRESHMENT AND THE INN

GARDEN AND ORCHARD

MUSIC BENEATH A BRANCH

THE SEA AND THE RIVER

THE REDDENING LEAF

NIGHT AND THE STARS

A LITTLE COMPANY OF GOOD
COUNTRY PEOPLE

A HANDFUL OF PHILOSOPHY

THE RETURN

THE FAREWELL TO WINTER
AND THE TOWN

Come, spur away,
I have no patience for a longer stay,
But must go down,
And leave the chargeable noise of this great town.
I will the country see. . . .

Thomas Randolph.

Oh, day, if I squander a wavelet of thee,
A mite of my twelve hours' treasure,
The least of thy gazes or glances . . .
The shame fall on Asolo, mischief on me !
Thy long, blue, solemn hours serenely flowing,
Whence earth, we feel, gets steady help and good—
Thy fitful sunshine minutes, coming, going,
As if earth turned from work in gamesome mood,
All shall be mine ! . . .

Robert Browning (*Pippa Passes*).

O the gleesome saunter over fields and hillsides !
The leaves and flowers of the commonest weeds, the moist fresh
stillness of the woods,
The exquisite smell of the earth at daybreak, and all through
the forenoon.

Walt Whitman.

I wish people would come into the country on May Day, and
fix in town the first of November.

Horace Walpole.

The Meadows in Spring ◡ ◡ ◡

'TIS a dull sight
　　To see the year dying,
When winter winds
　Set the yellow wood sighing :
　　Sighing, oh ! sighing.

When such a time cometh,
　I do retire
Into an old room
　Beside a bright fire :
　　Oh, pile a bright fire !

And there I sit
　Reading old things,
Of knights and lorn damsels,
　While the wind sings—
　　Oh, drearily sings !

I never look out
　Nor attend to the blast ;

For all to be seen
   Is the leaves falling fast :
      Falling, falling !

But close at the hearth,
   Like a cricket, sit I.
Reading of summer
   And chivalry—
      Gallant chivalry !

Then with an old friend
   I talk of our youth—
How 'twas gladsome, but often
   Foolish, forsooth :
      But gladsome, gladsome !

Or to get merry
   We sing some old rhyme,
That made the wood ring again
   In summer time—
      Sweet summer time !

Then go we to smoking,
   Silent and snug :
Nought passes between us,
   Save a brown jug—
      Sometimes !

And sometimes a tear
   Will rise in each eye,

Seeing the two old friends
　So merrily—
　　So merrily !

And ere to bed
　Go we, go we,
Down on the ashes
　We kneel on the knee,
　　Praying together !

Thus, then, live I,
　Till, 'mid all the gloom,
By heaven ! the bold sun
　Is with me in the room
　　Shining, shining !

Then the clouds part,
　Swallows soaring between ;
The spring is alive,
　And the meadows are green !

I jump up, like mad,
　Break the old pipe in twain.
And away to the meadows,
　The meadows again !
　　　　　　　Edward FitzGerald

YONDER in the heather there's a bed for
    sleeping,
  Drink for one athirst, ripe blackberries to eat ;
Yonder in the sun the merry hares go leaping,
  And the pool is clear for travel-wearied feet.

Sorely throb my feet, a-tramping London highways,
  (Ah ! the springy moss upon a northern moor !)
Through the endless streets, the gloomy squares and
    byways,
  Homeless in the City, poor among the poor !

London streets are gold—ah, give me leaves a-
    glinting
  'Midst grey dykes and hedges in the autumn
    sun !
London water's wine, poured out for all unstinting—
  God ! For the little brooks that tumble as they
    run !

Oh, my heart is fain to hear the soft wind blowing,
  Soughing through the fir-tops up on northern
    fells !
Oh, my eye's an ache to see the brown burns flowing
  Through the peaty soil and tinkling heather-
    bells.

Ada Smith.

BEYOND the East the sunrise, beyond the West
the sea,

And East and West the wander-thirst that will not
let me be ;

It works in me like madness, dear, to bid me say
good-bye ;

For the seas call and the stars call, and oh ! the call
of the sky !

I know not where the white road runs, nor what the
blue hills are,

But a man can have the Sun for friend, and for his
guide a star ;

And there's no end of voyaging when once the voice
is heard,

For the river calls and the road calls, and oh ! the
call of a bird !

Yonder the long horizon lies, and there by night and
day

The old ships draw to home again, the young ships
- sail away ;

And come I may, but go I must, and if men ask you
why,

You may put the blame on the stars and the Sun and
the white road and the sky !

Gerald Gould.

I WILL arise and go now, and go to Innisfree,
  And a small cabin build there, of clay and
    wattles made ;
Nine bean rows will I have there, a hive for the
  honey bee,
  And live alone in the bee-loud glade.

And I shall have some peace there, for peace comes
    dropping slow,
  Dropping from the veils of the morning to where
    the cricket sings ;
There midnight's all a glimmer, and noon a purple
    glow,
  And evening full of the linnet's wings.

I will arise and go now, for always, night and day,
  I hear lake-water lapping with low sounds by the
    shore ;
While I stand on the roadway or on the pavements
    gray,
  I hear it in the deep heart's core.

W. B. Yeats.

BEST and brightest, come away,—
 Fairer far than this fair Day,
Which, like thee, to those in sorrow
Comes to bid a sweet good-morrow
To the rough year just awake
In its cradle on the brake.
The brightest hour of unborn Spring
Through the winter wandering,
Found, it seems, the halcyon morn
To hoar February born ;
Bending from Heaven, in azure mirth,
It kissed the forehead of the earth,
And smiled upon the silent sea,
And bade the frozen streams be free,
And waked to music all their fountains,
And breathed upon the frozen mountains,
And like a prophetess of May
Strewed flowers upon the barren way,
Making the wintry world appear
Like one on whom thou smilest, dear.

 Away, away, from men and towns,
To the wild wood and the downs—
To the silent wilderness
Where the soul need not repress
Its music, lest it should not find
An echo in another's mind,

While the touch of Nature's art
Harmonizes heart to heart.

Radiant Sister of the Day
Awake ! arise ! and come away !
To the wild woods and the plains,
To the pools where winter rains
Image all their roof of leaves,
Where the pine its garland weaves
Of sapless green, and ivy dun,
Round stems that never kiss the sun ;
Where the lawns and pastures be
And the sandhills of the sea ;
Where the melting hoar-frost wets
The daisy-star that never sets,
And wind-flowers and violets
Which yet join not scent to hue
Crown the pale year weak and new ;
When the night is left behind
In the deep east, dim and blind,
And the blue noon is over us,
And the multitudinous
Billows murmur at our feet,
Where the earth and ocean meet,
And all things seem only one
In the universal Sun.

Percy Bysshe Shelley.

The Early Morning

THE Moon on the one hand, the Dawn on the
    other ;
The Moon is my sister, the Dawn is my brother.
The Moon on my left, and the Dawn on my right ;
My Brother, good-morning ; my Sister, good-night.

Hilaire Belloc.

Mrs. Stuart's Retirement

FROM the Court to the Cottage convey me away !
    For I'm weary of grandeur, and what they call
       "gay" ;
       Where Pride without measure,
       And Pomp without pleasure,
Make life, in a circle of hurry, decay.

Far remote and retired from the noise of the Town ;
I'll exchange my brocade for a plain russet gown !
       My friends shall be few,
       But well chosen and true ;
And sweet recreation our evening shall crown !

With a rural repast, a rich banquet to me,
On a mossy green bank, near some shady old tree,
       The river's clear brink
       Shall afford me my drink ;
And Temp'rance my friendly Physician shall be !

Ever calm and serene, with contentment still blest,
Not too giddy with joy, or with sorrow deprest,
   I'll neither invoke,
    Nor repine at, Death's stroke !
But retire from the world, as I would to my rest.

Henry Carey.

THE ROAD

In its widest sense, "the open road" is the sign and symbol of all outdoor life, of all holiday-making in which the sense of the athlete is awakened,—in a word, of all that is active and adventurous, from sailing and rowing to cliff-climbing and moorland tramping. But fascinating as these are, there is a something even more fascinating in the thought of the open road when we narrow the meaning and confine it to the paths trod by the feet of men and horses and cut by their wheels—restrict it, that is, to those nerves and sinews of the soil which bind village to village, city to city, and land to land. Think of all the many and diverse tracks which, once landed at Calais, if only you keep going eastward, will take you to Moscow or Tobolsk, westward to Lisbon or Madrid, and southward to Rome. What is more intellectually exhilarating to the mind, and even to the senses, than to stand looking down the vista of some great road in France or Italy, or up a long and well-worn horse-track in Asia or Africa, a path which has not yet been trod by the foot or the wheel of the gazing wayfarer, or by the hoof of his horse, and to wonder through what strange places, by what towns and castles, by what rivers and streams, by what mountains and valleys it will take him ere he reaches his destination?

The Spectator.

Jog on, jog on the foot pathway,
 And merrily hent the stile-a,
Your merry heart goes all the day,
 Your sad heart tires in a mile-a.

Shakespeare.

I am told there are people who do not care for maps, and find it hard to believe. The names, the shapes of the woodlands, the courses of the roads and rivers, the prehistoric footsteps of man still distinctly traceable up hill and down dale, the mills and the ruins, the ponds and the ferries, perhaps the *Standing Stone* or the *Druidic Circle* on the heath ; here is an inexhaustible fund of interest for any man with eyes to see or twopence-worth of imagination to understand with !

R. L. Stevenson.

TITANIA. Peas-blossom! Cobweb! Moth! and
   Mustard-seed!

(*Enter four Fairies.*)

First Fairy. Ready.
Second Fairy. And I.
Third Fairy. And I.
Fourth Fairy. Where shall we go?
Titania. Be kind and courteous to this gentleman;
Hop in his walks, and gambol in his eyes;
Feed him with apricocks, and dewberries;
With purple grapes, green figs, and mulberries;
The honey bags steal from the humble bees,
And, for night-tapers, crop their waxen thighs,
And light them at the fiery glow-worm's eyes,
To have my love to bed, and to arise;
And pluck the wings from painted butterflies,
To fan the moonbeams from his sleeping eyes:
Nod to him, elves, and do him courtesies.

Shakespeare.

The Vagabond ✎ ✎ ✎ ✎

(To an air of Schubert)

GIVE to me the life I love,
    Let the lave go by me,
Give the jolly heaven above
    And the byway nigh me.
Bed in the bush with stars to see,
    Bread I dip in the river—
There's the life for a man like me,
    There's the life for ever.

Let the blow fall soon or late,
    Let what will be o'er me ;
Give the face of earth around
    And the road before me.
Wealth I seek not, hope nor love,
    Nor a friend to know me ;
All I seek, the heaven above
    And the road below me.

Or let autumn fall on me
    Where afield I linger,
Silencing the bird on tree,
    Biting the blue finger.
White as meal the frosty field—
    Warm the fireside haven—
Not to autumn will I yield,
    Not to winter even !

16

Let the blow fall soon or late,
    Let what will be o'er me ;
Give the face of earth around,
    And the road before me.
Wealth I ask not, hope nor love,
    Nor a friend to know me ;
All I ask, the heaven above
    And the road below me.

Robert Louis Stevenson.

The White Road up Athirt the Hill

WHEN high hot zuns da strik right down,
    An' burn our zweaty fiazen brown,
An' zunny hangèns that be nigh
Be back'd by hills so blue's the sky ;
Then while the bells da sweetly cheem
Upon the champèn high-neck'd team
How lively, wi' a friend, da seem
    The white road up athirt the hill.

The zwellèn downs, wi' chāky tracks,
A-climmèn up ther zunny backs,
Da hide green meäds, an' zedgy brooks,
An' clumps o' trees wi' glossy rooks,
An' hearty vo'ke to lafe and zing,
An' churches wi' ther bells to ring,
In parishes al in a string
    Wi' white roads up athirt the hills.

Àt feäst, when uncle's vo'ke da come
To spend the dā wi' we at huome,
An' we da put upon the buard
The best of al we can avvuord,
The wolden oons da tā'ke an' smoke,
An' younger oons da plāy an' joke,
An' in the evemen all our vo'ke
　　Da bring 'em gwáin athirt the hill.

Var thee the green da zwarm wi' wold
An' young so thick as sheep in vuold.
The billis in the blacksmith's shop
An' mēsh-green waterwheel da stop,
An' luonesome in the wheelwright's shed
's a-left the wheelless waggon bed,
While zwarms o' comen-friends da tread
　　The white road down athirt the hill.

An' when the windēn road so white
A-climmèn up the hill in zight,
Da leäd to pliazen, east ar west
The vust a-know'd an' lov'd the best,
How touchèn in the zunsheen's glow
Ar in the shiades that clouds da drow
Upon the zunburn'd down below,
　　's the white road up athirt the hill.

What pirty hollers now the long
White roads da windy roun' among,
Wi' diary cows in woody nooks,
An' hâymiakers among their pooks,

An' housen that the trees da screen
Vrom zun an' zight by boughs o' green,
Young blushèn beauty's huomes between
 The white roads up athirt the hills.
                                   William Barnes.

The Joys of the Road ⌒ ⌒ ⌒ ⌒

NOW the joys of the road are chiefly these :
 A crimson touch on the hard-wood trees ;

A vagrant's morning wide and blue,
In early fall, when the wind walks, too ;

A shadowy highway cool and brown,
Alluring up and enticing down

From rippled water to dappled swamp,
From purple glory to scarlet pomp ;

The outward eye, the quiet will,
And the striding heart from hill to hill ;

The tempter apple over the fence ;
The cobweb bloom on the yellow quince ;

The palish asters along the wood,—
A lyric touch of the solitude ;

An open hand, an easy shoe,
And a hope to make the day go through,—

Another to sleep with, and a third
To wake me up at the voice of a bird,

The resonant far-listening morn,
And the hoarse whisper of the corn ;

The crickets mourning their comrades lost,
In the night's retreat from the gathering frost ;

(Or is it their slogan, plaintive and shrill,
As they beat on their corselets, valiant still ?)

A hunger fit for the kings of the sea,
And a loaf of bread for Dickon and me ;

A thirst like that of the Thirsty Sword,
And a jug of cider on the board ;

An idle noon, a bubbling spring,
The sea in the pine-tops murmuring ;

A scrap of gossip at the ferry ;
A comrade neither glum nor merry,

Asking nothing, revealing naught,
But minting his words from a fund of thought,

A keeper of silence eloquent,
Needy, yet royally well content,

Of the mettled breed, yet abhorring strife,
And full of the mellow juice of life,

A taster of wine, with an eye for a maid.
Never too bold, and never afraid,

Never heart-whole, never heart-sick,
(These are the things I worship in Dick)

No fidget and no reformer, just
A calm observer of ought and must,

A lover of books, but a reader of man,
No cynic and no charlatan,

Who never defers and never demands,
But, smiling, takes the world in his hands,—

Seeing it good as when God first saw
And gave it the weight of His will for law.

And O the joy that is never won,
But follows and follows the journeying sun,

By marsh and tide, by meadow and stream,
A will-o'-the-wind, a light-o'-dream,

Delusion afar, delight anear,
From morrow to morrow, from year to year.

A jack-o'-lantern, a fairy fire,
A dare, a bliss, and a desire !

The racy smell of the forest loam,
When the stealthy, sad-heart leaves go home ;

(O leaves, O leaves, I am one with you,
Of the mould and the sun and the wind and the dew !)

The broad gold wake of the afternoon ;
The silent fleck of the cold new moon ;

The sound of the hollow sea's release
From stormy tumult to starry peace ;

With only another league to wend ;
And two brown arms at the journey's end !

These are the joys of the open road—
For him who travels without a load.

Bliss Carman.

Four Solaces

I. The Meadow at Noon.

HERE fling thyself down on the grassy meadow,
O traveller, and rest thy relaxed limbs from
painful weariness ; since here also, as thou listenest
to the cicalas' tune, the stone-pine trembling in the
wafts of west wind will lull thee, and the shepherd
on the mountains piping at noon nigh the spring
under a copse of leafy plane : so escaping the ardours
of the autumnal dogstar thou wilt cross the height
to-morrow ; trust this good counsel that Pan gives
thee.

Author unknown.

II. The Roadside Pool.

DRINK not here, traveller, from this warm pool in the brook, full of mud stirred by the sheep at pasture ; but go a very little way over the ridge where the heifers are grazing ; for there by yonder pastoral stone-pine thou wilt find bubbling through the fountained rock a spring colder than northern snow.

Leonidas of Tarentum.

III. The Orchard-Corner.

I, HERMES, stand here by the windy orchard in the cross-ways nigh the grey sea-shore, giving rest on the way to wearied men ; and the fountain wells forth cold stainless water.

Anyte.

IV. Hermes of the Ways.

GO and rest your limbs here for a little under the juniper, O wayfarers, by Hermes, Guardian of the Way, not in crowds, but those of you whose knees are tired with heavy toil and thirst after traversing a long road ; for there a breeze and a shady seat and the fountain under the rock will lull your toil-wearied limbs ; and having so escaped the midday breath of the autumnal dogstar, as is right, honour Hermes of the Ways.

Author unknown.

(J. W. Mackail's translation.)

23

THERE was a man was half a clown
    (It's so, my father tells of it),
He saw the church in Clermont Town,
    And laughed to hear the bells of it.

He laughed to hear the bells that ring
    In Clermont Church and round of it ;
He heard the verger's daughter sing,
    And loved her for the sound of it.

The verger's daughter said him nay
    (She had the right of choice in it) ;
He left the town at break of day
    (He hadn't had a voice in it).

   .   .   .   .   .

The road went up, the road went down,
    And there the matter ended it ;
He broke his heart in Clermont Town,
    At Pontgibaud they mended it.

                    Hilaire Belloc.

Song of the Open Road ᧬ ᧬ ᧬ ᧬

I

AFOOT and light-hearted I take to the open road,
    Healthy, free, the world before me,
The long brown path before me leading wherever I
choose.

Henceforth I ask not good-fortune, I myself am good-
fortune,
Henceforth I whimper no more, postpone no more,
need nothing,
Done with indoor complaints, libraries, querulous
criticisms,
Strong and content I travel the open road.

The earth, that is sufficient,
I do not want the constellations any nearer,
I know they are very well where they are,
I know they suffice for those who belong to them.

(Still here I carry my old delicious burdens,
I carry them, men and women, I carry them with me
wherever I go,
I swear it is impossible for me to get rid of them,
I am fill'd with them, and I will fill them in return.)

2

You road I enter upon and look around, I believe you
are not all that is here,
I believe that much unseen is also here.

Here the profound lesson of reception, nor preference
nor denial,
The black with his woolly head, the felon, the diseas'd,
the illiterate person, are not denied ;
The birth, the hasting after the physician, the beggar's
tramp, the drunkard's stagger, the laughing party
of mechanics,

The escaped youth, the rich person's carriage, the fop,
the eloping couple,
The early market-man, the hearse, the moving of
furniture into the town, the return back from the
town,
They pass, I also pass, any thing passes, none can be
interdicted,
None but are accepted, none but shall be dear to
me.

3

You air that serves me with breath to speak!
You objects that call from diffusion my meanings and
give them shape!
You light that wraps me and all things in delicate
equable showers!
You paths worn in the irregular hollows by the
roadsides!
I believe you are latent with unseen existences, you
are so dear to me.

You flagg'd walks of the cities! you strong curbs at
the edges!
You ferries! you planks and posts of wharves! you
timber-lined sides! you distant ships!
You rows of houses! you window-pierc'd façades!
you roofs!
You porches and entrances! you copings and iron
guards!

You windows whose transparent shells might expose
    so much !
You doors and ascending steps ! you arches !
You grey stones of interminable pavements ! you
    trodden crossings !
From all that has touch'd you I believe you have
    imparted to yourselves, and now would impart
    the same secretly to me,
From the living and the dead you have peopled your
    impassive surfaces, and the spirits thereof would
    be evident and amicable with me.

4

The earth expanding right hand and left hand,
The picture alive, every part in its best light,
The music falling in where it is wanted, and stopping
    where it is not wanted,
The cheerful voice of the public road, the gay fresh
    sentiment of the road.

O highway I travel, do you say to me *Do not leave
    me ?*
Do you say *Venture not—if you leave me you are
    lost ?*
Do you say *I am already prepared, I am well beaten
    and undenied, adhere to me ?*

O public road, I say back I am not afraid to leave
    you, yet I love you,
You express me better than I can express myself,
You shall be more to me than my poem.

I think heroic deeds were all conceiv'd in the open
    air, and all free poems also,
I think I could stop here myself and do miracles,
I think whatever I shall meet on the road I shall like,
    and whoever beholds me shall like me,
I think whoever I see must be happy.

5

From this hour I ordain myself loos'd of limits and
    imaginary lines,
Going where I list, my own master total and
    absolute,
Listening to others, considering well what they say,
Pausing, searching, receiving, contemplating,
Gently, but with undeniable will, divesting myself of
    the holds that would hold me.

I inhale great draughts of space,
The east and the west are mine, and the north and
    the south are mine.

I am larger, better than I thought,
I did not know I held so much goodness.

All seems beautiful to me,
I can repeat over to men and women You have done
    such good to me I would do the same to you,
I will recruit for myself and you as I go,
I will scatter myself among men and women as I
    go,

I will toss a new gladness and roughness among
them,
Whoever denies me it shall not trouble me,
Whoever accepts me he or she shall be blessed and
shall bless me.

6

Now if a thousand perfect men were to appear it
would not amaze me,
Now if a thousand beautiful forms of women appear'd
it would not astonish me.
Now I see the secret of the making of the best
persons,
It is to grow in the open air and to eat and sleep with
the earth.

Here a great personal deed has room,
(Such a deed seizes upon the hearts of the whole race
of men,
Its effusion of strength and will overwhelms laws and
mocks all authority and all argument against it).

Here is the test of wisdom :
Wisdom is not finally tested in schools,
Wisdom cannot be pass'd from one having it to
another not having it,
Wisdom is of the soul, is not susceptible of proof, is
its own proof,
Applies to all stages and objects and qualities and is
content,

Is the certainty of the reality and immortality of
    things, and the excellence of things ;
Something there is in the float of the sight of things
    that provokes it out of the soul.

Now I re-examine philosophies and religions,
They may prove well in lecture-rooms, yet not prove
    at all under the spacious clouds and along the
    landscape and flowing currents.

Here is realisation,
Here is a man tallied—he realises here what he has
    in him,
The past, the future, majesty, love—if they are vacant
    of you, you are vacant of them.

Only the kernel of every object nourishes ;
Where is he who tears off the husks for you and me ?
Where is he that undoes stratagems and envelopes
    for you and me ?

Here is adhesiveness, it is not previously fashion'd,
    it is apropos ;
Do you know what it is as you pass to be loved by
    strangers ?
Do you know the talk of those turning eye-balls ?

7

Here is the efflux of the soul,
The efflux of the soul comes from within through
    embower'd gates, ever provoking questions,

These yearnings, why are they? these thoughts in the
    darkness, why are they?
Why are there men and women that while they are
    nigh me the sunlight expands my blood?
Why when they leave me do my pennants of joy sink
    flat and lank?
Why are there trees I never walk under but large and
    melodious thoughts descend upon me?
(I think they hang there winter and summer on those
    trees and always drop fruit as I pass;)
What is it I interchange so suddenly with strangers?
What with some driver as I ride on the seat by his
    side?
What with some fisherman drawing his seine by the
    shore as I walk by and pause?
What gives me to be free to a woman's and man's
    good-will? what gives them to be free to mine?

8

The efflux of the soul is happiness, here is happiness,
I think it pervades the open air, waiting at all times,
Now it flows unto us, we are rightly charged.

Here rises the fluid and attaching character,
The fluid and attaching character is the freshness and
    sweetness of man and woman,
(The herbs of the morning sprout no fresher and
    sweeter every day out of the roots of themselves,
    than it sprouts fresh and sweet continually out of
    itself).

31

Toward the fluid and attaching character exudes the
    sweat of the love of young and old,
From it falls distill'd the charm that mocks beauty
    and attainments,
Toward it heaves the shuddering longing ache of
    contact.

9

Allons! Whoever you are, come travel with me!
Travelling with me you find what never tires.

The earth never tires,
The earth is rude, silent, incomprehensible at first,
    Nature is rude and incomprehensible at first,
Be not discouraged, keep on, there are divine things
    well envelop'd,
I swear to you there are divine things more beautiful
    than words can tell.

Allons! we must not stop here,
However sweet these laid-up stores, however con-
    venient this dwelling, we cannot remain here,
However shelter'd this port and however calm these
    waters, we must not anchor here,
However welcome the hospitality that surrounds us,
    we are permitted to receive it but a little while.

10

Allons! the inducements shall be greater,
We will sail pathless and wild seas,
We will go where winds blow, waves dash, and the
    Yankee clipper speeds by under full sail.

Allons ! with power, liberty, the earth, the elements,
Health, defiance, gaiety, self-esteem, curiosity ;
Allons ! from all formules !
From your formules, O bat-eyed and materialistic
    priests.

The stale cadaver blocks up the passage—the burial
    waits no longer.

Allons ! yet take warning !
He travelling with me needs the best blood, thews,
    endurance,
None may come to the trial till he or she bring
    courage and health,
Come not here if you have already spent the best of
    yourself,
Only those may come who come in sweet and deter-
    min'd bodies,
No diseas'd person, no rum drinker or venereal taint
    is permitted here.
(I and mine do not convince by arguments, similes,
    rhymes,
We convince by our presence.)

11

Listen ! I will be honest with you :
I do not offer the old smooth prizes, but offer rough
    new prizes,
These are the days that must happen to you :

You shall not heap up what is call'd riches,

You shall scatter with lavish hand all that you earn or achieve,

You but arrive at the city to which you were destin'd, you hardly settle yourself to satisfaction before you are call'd by an irresistible call to depart,

You shall be treated to the ironical smiles and mockings of those who remain behind you,

What beckonings of love you receive you shall only answer with passionate kisses of parting,

You shall not allow the hold of those who spread their reach'd hands toward you.

12

Allons! after the great Companions, and to belong to them!

They too are on the road — they are the swift and majestic men—they are the greatest women,

Enjoyers of calms of seas and storms of seas,

Sailors of many a ship, walkers of many a mile of land,

Habitués of many distant countries, habitués of far distant dwellings,

Trusters of men and women, observers of cities, solitary toilers,

Pausers and contemplators of tufts, blossoms, shells of the shore,

Dancers at wedding-dances, kissers of brides, tender helpers of children, bearers of children,

Soldiers of revolts, standers by gaping graves,
lowerers-down of coffins,
Journeyers over consecutive seasons, over the years,
the curious years each emerging from that which
preceded it,
Journeyers as with companions, namely their own
diverse phases,
Forth-steppers from the latent unrealised baby-days,
Journeyers gaily with their own youth, journeyers
with their bearded and well-grain'd manhood,
Journeyers with their womanhood, ample, unsur-
pass'd, content,
Journeyers with their own sublime old age, of manhood or womanhood,
Old age, calm, expanded, broad with the haughty
breadth of the universe,
Old age, flowing free with the delicious near-by
freedom of death.

13

Allons! to that which is endless as it was begin-
ningless,
To undergo much, tramps of days, rests of nights,
To merge all in the travel they tend to, and the days
and nights they tend to,
Again to merge them in the start of superior journeys,
To see nothing anywhere but what you may reach it
and pass it,
To conceive no time, however distant, but what you
may reach it and pass it,

To look up or down no road but it stretches and waits
for you, however long but it stretches and waits
for you,

To see no being, not God's or any, but you also go
thither,

To see no possession but you may possess it, enjoying
all without labour or purchase, abstracting the
feast yet not abstracting one particle of it,

To take the best of the farmer's farm and the rich
man's elegant villa, and the chaste blessings of
the well-married couple, and the fruits of orchards
and flowers of gardens,

To take to your use out of the compact cities as you
pass through,

To carry buildings and streets with you afterward
wherever you go,

To gather the minds of men out of their brains as you
encounter them, to gather the love out of their
hearts,

To take your lovers on the road with you, for all that
you leave them behind you,

To know the universe itself as a road, as many roads,
as roads for travelling souls.

All parts away for the progress of souls,

All religion, all solid things, arts, governments—all
that was or is apparent upon this globe or any
globe, falls into niches and corners before the
procession of souls along the grand roads of the
universe.

Of the progress of the souls of men and women along
    the grand roads of the universe, all other progress
    is the needed emblem and sustenance.

Forever alive, forever forward,
Stately, solemn, sad, withdrawn, baffled, mad, turbulent,
    feeble, dissatisfied,
Desperate, proud, fond, sick, accepted by men, rejected
    by men,
They go! they go! I know that they go, but I know
    not where they go,
But I know that they go toward the best—toward
    something great.

Whoever you are, come forth! or man or woman,
    come forth!
You must not stay sleeping and dallying there in the
    house, though you built it, or though it has been
    built for you.

Out of the dark confinement! out from behind the
    screen!
It is useless to protest, I know all and expose it.

Behold through you as bad as the rest,
Through the laughter, dancing, dining, supping, of
    people,
Inside of dresses and ornaments, inside of those
    wash'd and trimm'd faces,
Behold a secret silent loathing and despair.

No husband, no wife, no friend, trusted to hear the confession,

Another self, a duplicate of every one, skulking and hiding it goes,

Formless and wordless through the streets of the cities, polite and bland in the parlours,

In the cars of railroads, in steamboats, in the public assembly,

Home to the houses of men and women, at the table, in the bed-room, everywhere,

Smartly attired, countenance smiling, form upright, death under the breast-bones, hell under the skull-bones,

Under the broadcloth and gloves, under the ribbons and artificial flowers,

Keeping fair with the customs, speaking not a syllable of itself.

Speaking of any thing else, but never of itself.

14

Allons ! through struggles and wars !

The goal that was named cannot be countermanded.

Have the past struggles succeeded ?

What has succeeded ? yourself ? your nation ? Nature ?

Now understand me well—it is provided in the essence of things that from any fruition of success, no matter what, shall come forth something to make a greater struggle necessary.

My call is the call of battle, I nourish active rebellion,
He going with me must go well arm'd,
He going with me goes often with spare diet, poverty,
    angry enemies, desertions.

15

Allons ! the road is before us !
It is safe—I have tried it—my own feet have tried it
    well—be not detain'd !
Let the paper remain on the desk unwritten, and the
    book on the shelf unopen'd !
Let the tools remain in the workshop ! let the money
    remain unearn'd !
Let the school stand ! mind not the cry of the teacher !
Let the preacher preach in his pulpit ! let the lawyer
    plead in the court, and the judge expound the
    law.

Camerado, I will give you my hand !
I give you my love more precious than money,
I give you myself before preaching or law ;
Will you give me yourself ? will you come travel with
    me ?
Shall we stick by each other as long as we live ?
Walt Whitman.

LONG is the road 'twixt town and town that runs,
  Travelled by many a lordly cavalcade,
With trappings gay, and rich caparisons,
  Jester and squire, and laughing knight and maid:
With gallant clash and stir they go their way:
I trudge afoot thro' all the drouth of day.

For me, the misty meadows fresh with morn,
  The tramp thro' noontide heat to evening gray,
The far-seen smoke from the day's goal upborne,
  The halt, the friendly greeting by the way,
The distant hill behind far hill descried,
The road by day, the rest at eventide.

I know each wayside wood, each moorland brown,
  Each hidden byway and reposeful nook,
Where I may linger when the sun goes down,
  Dipping tired feet in some cool flowing brook;
I know the free hill and the glooming glen,
And kindly fires, and humble homes of men.

                                    C. Fox Smith.

SPRING AND THE BEAUTY
OF THE EARTH

Sweetest Earth, I love and love thee,
Seas about thee, skies above thee,
    Sun and storms,
    Hues and forms
Of the clouds with floating shadows
On thy mountains and thy meadows.

Earth, there's none that can enslave thee,
Not thy lords it is that have thee:
    Not for gold
    Art thou sold,
But thy lovers at their pleasure
Take thy beauty and thy treasure.

Margaret L. Woods.

Unnumber'd cottages and farms
That have for musing minds unnumber'd charms.

George Crabbe.

One passage in your letter a little displeas'd me. The rest
was nothing but kindness, which Robert's letters are ever
brimful of. You say that "this World to you seems drain'd
of all its sweets!" At first I had hoped you only meant to
intimate the high price of Sugar! but I am afraid you meant
more. O, Robert, I don't know what you call sweet. Honey
and the honeycomb, roses and violets, are yet in the earth.
The sun and moon yet reign in Heaven, and the lesser lights
keep up their pretty twinklings. Meats and drinks, sweet
sights and sweet smells, a country walk, spring and autumn,
follies and repentance, quarrels and reconcilements, have all a
sweetness by turns. Good humour and good nature, friends at
home that love you, and friends abroad that miss you—you
possess all these things, and more innumerable, and these
are all sweet things. You may extract honey from everything.

Charles Lamb to Robert Lloyd.

Turn o' the Year

THIS is the time when bit by bit
　　The days begin to lengthen sweet,
And every minute gained is joy—
And love stirs in the heart of a boy.

This is the time the sun, of late
Content to lie abed till eight,
Lifts up betimes his sleepy head—
And love stirs in the heart of a maid.

This is the time we dock the night
Of a whole hour of candlelight ;
When song of linnet and thrush is heard—
And love stirs in the heart of a bird.

This is the time when sword-blades green,
With gold and purple damascene,
Pierce the brown crocus-bed a-row—
And love stirs in a heart I know.

Katharine Tynan Hinkson.

OUT of the veins of the world comes the blood of
    me ;
The heart that beats in my side is the heart of the sea ;
The hills have known me of old, and they do not
    forget ;
Long ago was I friends with the wind ; I am friends
    with it yet.

The hills are grey, they are strange ; they breed desire
Of a tune that the feet may march to and not tire ;
For always up in the distance the thin roads wind,
And passing out of sight, they pass not out of mind.

I am glad when morning and evening alter the skies ;
There speaks no voice of the stars but my voice
    replies ;
When wave on wave all night cries out in its need,
I listen, I understand ; my heart takes heed.

Out of the red-brown earth, out of the grey-brown
    streams,
Came this perilous body, cage of perilous dreams ;
To the ends of all waters and lands they are tossed,
    they are whirled,
For my dreams are one with my body, yea, one with
    the world.

Gerald Gould.

WHEN wintry weather's al a-done
    An' brooks da sparkle in the zun,
An' nâisy buildèn rooks da vlee
Wi' sticks toward ther elem tree,
An' we can hear birds zing, and zee
    Upon the boughs the buds o' spring,
    Then I don't envy any king,
        A-vield wi' health an' zunsheen.

Var then the cowslip's hangèn flow'r,
A-wetted in the zunny show'r,
Da grow wi' vilets sweet o' smell,
That mâidens al da like so well ;
An' drushes' aggs, wi' sky-blue shell,
    Da lie in mossy nests among
    The tharns, while thē da zing ther zong
        At evemen in.the zunsheen.

An' God da miake His win' to blow
An' râin to val var high an' low,
An' tell His marnen zun to rise
Var al alik' ; an' groun' an' skies
Ha' colors var the poor man's eyes ;
    An' in our trials He is near
    To hear our muoan an' zee our tear,
        An' turn our clouds to zunsheen.

An' many times, when I da vind
Things goo awry, and vo'ke unkind ;

To zee the quiet veedèn herds,
An' hear the zingèn o' the birds,
Da still my spurrit muore than words.
    Var I da zee that 'tis our sin
    Da miake oon's soul so dark 'ithin
        When God wood gie us zunsheen.

William Barnes.

April

APRIL, April,
    Laugh thy girlish laughter;
Then, the moment after,
Weep thy girlish tears!
April, that mine ears
Like a lover greetest,
If I tell thee, sweetest,
All my hopes and fears,
April, April,
Laugh thy golden laughter,
But, the moment after,
Weep thy golden tears!

William Watson.

In Early Spring

O SPRING, I know thee!   Seek for sweet surprise
    In the young children's eyes.
But I have learnt the years, and know the yet
    Leaf-folded violet.

Mine ear, awake to silence, can foretell
   The cuckoo's fitful bell.
I wander in a grey time that encloses
   June and the wild hedge-roses.
A year's procession of the flowers doth pass
   My feet, along the grass.
And all you sweet birds silent yet, I know
   The notes that stir you so,
Your songs yet half devised in the dim dear
   Beginnings of the year.
In these young days you meditate your part ;
   I have it all by heart.

I know the secrets of the seeds of flowers
   Hidden and warm with showers,
And how, in kindling Spring, the cuckoo shall
   Alter his interval.
But not a flower or song I ponder is
   My own, but memory's.
I shall be silent in those days desired
   Before a world inspired.
O dear brown birds, compose your old song-phrases,
   Earth, thy familiar daisies.

The poet mused upon the dusky height,
   Between two stars towards night,
His purpose in his heart.   I watched, a space,
   The meaning of his face :
There was the secret, fled from earth and skies,
   Hid in his grey young eyes.

47

My heart and all the Summer wait his choice,
  And wonder for his voice.
Who shall foretell his songs, and who aspire
  But to divine his lyre?
Sweet earth, we know thy dimmest mysteries,
  But he is lord of his.

Alice Meynell.

Song   ∽   ∽   ∽   ∽   ∽

THE year's at the spring
      And day's at the morn;
Morning's at seven;
The hill-side's dew-pearled;
The lark's on the wing;
The snail's on the thorn:
God's in His heaven—
All's right with the world!

Robert Browning.

Lynton Verses   ∽   ∽   ∽   ∽   ∽

SWEET breeze that sett'st the summer birds
      a-swaying,
Dear lambs amid the primrose meadows playing,
    Let me not think!
    O floods upon whose brink
  The merry birds are maying,

48

Dream, softly dream! O blessed mother, lead me
Unsevered from thy girdle—lead me! feed me!
   I have no will but thine ;
     I need not but the juice
   Of elemental wine—
     Perish remoter use
Of strength reserved for conflict yet to come !
Let me be dumb,
   As long as I may feel thy hand—
    This, this is all—do ye not understand
How the great Mother mixes all our bloods?
  O breeze ! O swaying buds !
  O lambs, O primroses, O floods !
            Thomas Edward Brown.

Home Thoughts from Abroad

OH, to be in England now that April's there,
    And whoever wakes in England sees, some
       morning unaware,
That the lowest boughs and the brushwood sheaf
Round the elm-tree bole are in tiny leaf,
While the chaffinch sings on the orchard bough
In England—now !
And after April, when May follows
And the white-throat builds, and all the swallows !
Hark, where my blossomed pear-tree in the hedge
Leans to the field and scatters on the clover
Blossoms and dewdrops—at the bent spray's edge—
That's the wise thrush : he sings each song twice over

D   49

Lest you should think he never could recapture
The first fine careless rapture !
And, though the fields look rough with hoary dew,
All will be gay when noontide wakes anew
The buttercups, the little children's dower
—Far brighter than this gaudy melon-flower !

Robert Browning.

A May Burden

THROUGH meadow-ways as I did tread,
  The corn grew in great lustihead,
And hey ! the beeches burgeonéd.
    By Goddés fay, by Goddés fay !
  It is the month, the jolly month,
  It is the jolly month of May.

God ripe the wines and corn, I say,
And wenches for the marriage-day,
And boys to teach love's comely play.
    By Goddés fay, by Goddés fay !
  It is the month, the jolly month,
  It is the jolly month of May.

As I went down by lane and lea,
The daisies reddened so, pardie !
" Blushets ! " I said, " I well do see,
    By Goddés fay, by Goddés fay !
  The thing ye think of in this month,
  Heigho ! this jolly month of May."

As down I went by rye and oats,
The blossoms smelt of kisses ; throats
Of birds turned kisses into notes ;
    By Goddés fay, by Goddés fay !
The kiss it is a growing flower,
I trow, this jolly month of May.

God send a mouth to every kiss,
Seeing the blossom of this bliss
By gathering doth grow, certes !
    By Goddés fay, by Goddés fay !
Thy brow-garland pushed all aslant
Tells—but I tell not, wanton May !

Francis Thompson.

Corrymeela

OVER here in England I'm helpin' wi' the hay,
    An' I wisht I was in Ireland the livelong day ;
Weary on the English hay, an' sorra take the wheat !
Och ! Corrymeela an' the blue sky over it.

There's a deep dumb river flowin' by beyont the
    heavy trees,
    This livin' air is moithered wi' the bummin' o' the
    bees ;
I wisht I'd hear the Claddagh burn go runnin' through
    the heat
    Past Corrymeela, wi' the blue sky over it.

The people that's in England is richer nor the Jews,
  There not the smallest young gossoon but thravels
    in his shoes !
I'd give the pipe between me teeth to see a barefut
  child,
    Och ! Corrymeela an' the low south wind.

Here's hands so full o' money an' hearts so full o'
  care,
    By the luck o' love ! I'd still go light for all I did
      go bare.
" God save ye, *colleen dhas,*" I said : the girl she
  thought me wild.
    Far Corrymeela, an' the low south wind.

D'ye mind me now, the song at night is mortial hard
  to raise,
    The girls are heavy goin' here, the boys are ill to
      plase ;
When onest I'm out this workin' hive, 'tis I'll be
  back again—
    Ay, Corrymeela, in the same soft rain.

The puff o' smoke from one ould roof before an
  English town !
    For a *shaugh* wid Andy Feelan here I'd give a
      silver crown,
For a curl o' hair like Mollie's ye'll ask the like in
  vain,
    Sweet Corrymeela, an' the same soft rain.
                                    Moira O'Neill.

AND when at last
Escaped, so many a green slope built on slope
Betwixt me and the enemy's house behind,
I dared to rest, or wander, in a rest
Made sweeter for the step upon the grass,
And view the ground's most gentle dimplement
(As if God's finger touched but did not press
In making England) such an up and down
Of verdure,—nothing too much up or down,
A ripple of land ; such little hills, the sky
Can stoop to tenderly and the wheatfields climb ;
Such nooks of valleys lined with orchises,
Fed full of noises by invisible streams ;
And open pastures where you scarcely tell
White daisies from white dew,—at intervals
The mythic oaks and elm-trees standing out
Self-poised upon their prodigy of shade,—
I thought my father's land was worthy too
Of being my Shakespeare's.

   · · · · · ·

Breaking into voluble ecstasy
I flattered all the beauteous country round,
As poets use, the skies, the clouds, the fields,
The happy violets hiding from the roads
The primroses run down to, carrying gold ;
The tangled hedgerows, where the cows push out
Impatient horns and tolerant churning mouths

'Twixt dripping ash-boughs,—hedgerows all alive
With birds and gnats and large white butter-
    flies
Which look as if the May-flower had caught
    life
And palpitated forth upon the wind ;
Hills, vales, woods, netted in a silver mist,
Farms, granges, doubled up among the hills ;
And cattle grazing in the watered vales,
And cottage-chimneys smoking from the woods,
And cottage-gardens smelling everywhere,
Confused with smell of orchards.

Elizabeth Barrett Browning.

England

SHOULDERS of upland brown laid dark to the
    sunset's bosom,
  Living amber of wheat, and copper of new-ploughed
    loam,
Downs where the white sheep wander, little gardens
    in blossom,
  Roads that wind through the twilight up to the
    lights of home.
Lanes that are white with hawthorn, dykes where the
    sedges shiver,
  Hollows where caged winds slumber, moorlands
  where winds wake free,

Sowing and reaping and gleaning, spring and torrent
and river,
　Are they not more, by worlds, than the whole of the
　　world can be?
Is there a corner of land, a furze-fringed rag of a
by-way,
　Coign of your foam-white cliffs or swirl of your
　　grass-green waves,
Leaf of your peaceful copse, or dust of your strenuous
highway,
　But in our hearts is sacred, dear as our cradles, our
　　graves?
Is not each bough in your orchards, each cloud in the
skies above you,
　Is not each byre or homestead, furrow or farm
　　or fold,
Dear as the last dear drops of the blood in the hearts
that love you,
　Filling those hearts till the love is more than the
　　heart can hold?

E. Nesbit.

(Italy Sweet too!　◇　◇　◇　◇　◇

HAPPY is England! I could be content
　　To see no other verdure than its own;
　　To feel no other breezes than are blown
Through its tall woods with high romances blent:

55

Yet do I sometimes feel a languishment
    For skies Italian, and an inward groan
    To sit upon an Alp as on a throne,
And half forget what world or worldling meant.

Happy is England, sweet her artless daughters ;
    Enough their simple loveliness for me,
        Enough their whitest arms in silence clinging :
    Yet do I often warmly burn to see
        Beauties of deeper glance, and hear their
            singing,
And float with them about the summer waters.

John Keats.)

Beauty Triumphant   ✐   ✐   ✐   ✐

A THING of beauty is a joy for ever :
    Its loveliness increases ; it will never
Pass into nothingness ; but still will keep
A bower quiet for us, and a sleep
Full of sweet dreams, and health, and quiet breathing.
Therefore, on every morrow, are we wreathing
A flowery band to bind us to the earth,
Spite of despondence, of the inhuman dearth
Of noble natures, of the gloomy days,
Of all the unhealthy and o'er-darken'd ways
Made for our searching : yes, in spite of all,
Some shape of beauty moves away the pall
From our dark spirits.   Such the sun, the moon,
Trees old and young, sprouting a shady boon

For simple sheep ; and such are daffodils
With the green world they live in ; and clear rills
That for themselves a cooling covert make
'Gainst the hot season ; the mid forest brake,
Rich with a sprinkling of fair musk-rose blooms :
And such too is the grandeur of the dooms
We have imagined for the mighty dead ;
All lovely tales that we have heard or read :
An endless fountain of immortal drink,
Pouring unto us from the heaven's brink.

John Keats.

"Cuttin' Rushes" ∽ ∽ ∽ ∽ ∽

OH maybe it was yesterday, or fifty years ago !
    Meself was risin' early on a day for cuttin'
    rushes,
Walkin' up the Brabla' burn, still the sun was low,
  Now I'd hear the burn run an' then I'd hear the
    thrushes.
Young, still young !—an' drenchin' wet the grass,
  Wet the golden honeysuckle hangin' sweetly down;
Here, lad, here ! will ye follow where I pass,
  An' find me cuttin' rushes on the mountain.

Then was it only yesterday, or fifty years or so?
  Rippin' round the bog pools high among the
    heather,

The hook it made me hand sore, I had to leave it go,
  'Twas he that cut the rushes then for me to bind
    together.
Come, dear, come!—an' back along the burn
  See the darlin' honeysuckle hangin' like a crown.
Quick, one kiss,—sure, there's someone at the turn !
  " Oh, we're afther cuttin' rushes on the mountain."

Yesterday, yesterday, or fifty years ago. . . .
  I waken out o' dreams when I hear the summer
    thrushes.
Oh, that's the Brabla' burn, I can hear it sing an' flow,
  For all that's fair, I'd sooner see a bunch o' green
    rushes.
Run, burn, run! can ye mind when we were young?
  The honeysuckle hangs above, the pool is dark an'
    brown :
Sing, burn, sing! an ye mind the song ye sung
  The day we cut the rushes on the mountain?
                                      Moira O'Neill.

Nature and Humanity   ∽   ∽   ∽   ∽

F OR nature then
(The coarser pleasures of my boyish days,
And their glad animal movements all gone by)
To me was all in all.—I cannot paint
What then I was.   The sounding cataract
Haunted me like a passion : the tall rock,

58

The mountain, and the deep and gloomy wood,
Their colours and their forms, were then to me
An appetite ; a feeling and a love,
That had no need of a remoter charm,
By thought supplied, nor any interest
Unborrowed from the eye.—That time is past,
And all its aching joys are now no more,
And all its dizzy raptures.   Not for this
Faint I, nor mourn nor murmur ; other gifts
Have followed ; for such loss, I would believe,
Abundant recompense.   For I have learned
To look on nature, not as in the hour
Of thoughtless youth ; but hearing oftentimes
The still, sad music of humanity,
Nor harsh nor grating, though of ample power
To chasten and subdue.   And I have felt
A presence that disturbs me with the joy
Of elevated thoughts : a sense sublime
Of something far more deeply interfused,
Whose dwelling is the light of setting suns,
And the round ocean and the living air,
And the blue sky, and in the mind of man :
A motion and a spirit, that impels
All thinking things, all objects of all thought,
And rolls through all things.   Therefore am I still
A lover of the meadows and the woods,
And mountains ; and of all that we behold
From this green earth ; of all the mighty world
Of eye and ear, both what they half create,
And what perceive ; well pleased to recognise

In nature and the language of the sense,
The anchor of my purest thoughts, the nurse,
The guide, the guardian of my heart, and soul
Of all my moral being.

William Wordsworth.

Hymn of Pan

FROM the forests and highlands
        We come, we come ;
From the river-girt islands,
        Where loud waves are dumb
            Listening to my sweet pipings.
The wind in the reeds and the rushes,
        The bees on the bells of thyme,
The birds on the myrtle bushes,
        The cicale above in the lime,
And the lizards below in the grass,
Were as silent as ever old Tmolus was,
        Listening to my sweet pipings.

Liquid Peneus was flowing,
        And all dark Tempe lay
In Pelion's shadow, outgrowing
        The light of the dying day,
            Speeded by my sweet pipings.
The Sileni, and Sylvans, and Fauns,
        And the Nymphs of the woods and waves,
To the edge of the moist river-lawns,
        And the brink of the dewy caves,

And all that did then attend and follow,
Were silent with love, as you now, Apollo,
    With envy of my sweet pipings.

I sang of the dancing stars,
    I sang of the dædal Earth,
And of Heaven—and the giant wars,
    And Love, and Death, and Birth,—
      And then I changed my pipings,—
Singing how down the vale of Menalus
    I pursued a maiden and clasped a reed :
Gods and men, we are all deluded thus !
    It breaks in our bosom and then we bleed :
All wept, as I think both ye now would,
If envy or age had not frozen your blood,
    At the sorrow of my sweet pipings.
              Percy Bysshe Shelley.

Pan's Piping

BREATHE music, O Pan that goest on the mountains, with thy sweet lips, breathe delight into thy pastoral reed, pouring song from the musical pipe, and make the melody sound in tune with the choral words ; and about thee to the pulse of the rhythm let the inspired foot of these water-nymphs keep falling free.

        Alcaeus of Messene.
      (J. W. Mackail's translation.)

THROUGH the black, rushing smoke-bursts,
  Thick breaks the red flame.
All Etna heaves fiercely
Her forest-clothed frame.

Not here, O Apollo !
Are haunts meet for thee.
But, where Helicon breaks down
In cliff to the sea.

Where the moon-silver'd inlets
Send far their light voice
Up the still vale of Thisbe,
O speed, and rejoice !

On the sward, at the cliff-top,
Lie strewn the white flocks ;
On the cliff-side the pigeons
Roost deep in the rocks.

In the moonlight the shepherds
Soft lull'd by the rills,
Lie wrapt in their blankets,
Asleep on the hills.

—What Forms are these coming
So white through the gloom ?
What garments out-glistening
The gold-flower'd broom ?

62

What sweet-breathing Presence
Out-perfumes the thyme?
What voices enrapture
The night's balmy prime?—

'Tis Apollo comes leading
His choir, the Nine.
—The Leader is fairest,
But all are divine.

They are lost in the hollows!
They stream up again!
What seeks on this mountain
The glorified train?—

They bathe on this mountain,
In the spring by their road;
Then on to Olympus,
Their endless abode.

—Whose praise do they mention?
Of what is it told?—
What will be for ever;
What was from of old.

First hymn they the Father
Of all things; and then,
The rest of Immortals,
The action of men.

The Day in its hotness,
The strife with the palm ;
The Night in its silence,
The Stars in their calm.

Matthew Arnold.

Bacchus ∽ ∽ ∽ ∽ ∽ ∽

AND as I sat, over the light blue hills
    There came a noise of revellers : the rills
Into the wide stream came of purple hue—
    'Twas Bacchus and his crew !
The earnest trumpet spake, and silver thrills
From kissing cymbals made a merry din—
    'Twas Bacchus and his kin !
Like to a moving vintage down they came,
Crown'd with green leaves, and faces all on flame ;
All madly dancing through the pleasant valley,
    To scare thee, Melancholy !

John Keats.

THE LOVER SINGS

When I walk by myself alone
It doth me good my songs to render.

William Wager.

The sun it goes down, the sky it looks red,
On yonder pillow I lay down my head,
I lift up my eyes to see the stars shine,
But still this young damsel she runs in my mind.

Old Sussex Song.

Song

HOW sweet I roamed from field to field,
   And tasted all the summer's pride
Till I the Prince of Love beheld
   Who in the sunny beams did glide !

He shewed me lilies for my hair,
   And blushing roses for my brow ;
He led me through his gardens fair
   Where all his golden pleasures grow.

With sweet May-dews my wings were wet,
   And Phœbus fired my vocal rage ;
He caught me in his silken net,
   And shut me in his golden cage.

He loves to sit and hear me sing ;
   Then, laughing, sports and plays with me ;
Then stretches out my golden wing,
   And mocks my loss of liberty.

William Blake.

Song

MY true-love hath my heart, and I have his,
  By just exchange one to the other given :
I hold his dear, and mine he cannot miss,—
There never was a better bargain driven :
  My true-love hath my heart, and I have his.

His heart in me keeps him and me in one,
My heart in him his thoughts and senses guides :
He loves my heart, for once it was his own,
I cherish his because in me it bides :
  My true-love hath my heart, and I have his.

Sir Philip Sidney.

Song

O MISTRESS mine, where are you roaming ?
  O, stay and hear ; your true Love's coming,
  That can sing both high and low :
Trip no further, pretty Sweeting ;
Journeys end in lovers' meeting,
  Every wise man's son doth know.

What is love ? 'tis not hereafter ;
Present mirth hath present laughter ;
  What's to come is still unsure :
In delay there lies no plenty :
Then come kiss me, Sweet-and-twenty,
  Youth's a stuff will not endure.

William Shakespeare.

Song

LET my voice ring out and over the earth,
   Through all the grief and strife,
With a golden joy in a silver mirth :
   Thank God for Life !

Let my voice swell out through the great abyss
   To the azure dome above,
With a chord of faith in the harp of bliss :
   Thank God for Love !

Let my voice thrill out beneath and above,
   The whole world through :
O my Love and Life, O my Life and Love,
   Thank God for you !

James Thomson.

Song

OH, like a queen's her happy tread
   And like a queen's her golden head !
But oh, at last, when all is said,
   Her woman's heart for me !

We wandered where the river gleamed
'Neath oaks that mused and pines that dreamed.
A wild thing of the woods she seemed,
   So proud, and pure, and free !

69

All heaven drew nigh to hear her sing,
When from her lips her soul took wing ;
The oaks forgot their pondering,
    The pines their reverie.

And oh, her happy queenly tread,
And oh, her queenly golden head !
But oh, her heart, when all is said,
    Her woman's heart for me !

                    William Watson.

The Lady of the Lambs ⌒ ⌒ ⌒ ⌒

SHE walks—the lady of my delight—
    A shepherdess of sheep.
Her flocks are thoughts.   She keeps them white ;
  She guards them from the steep.
She feeds them on the fragrant height,
  And folds them in for sleep.

She roams maternal hills and bright,
  Dark valleys safe and deep.
Her dreams are innocent at night ;
  The chastest stars may peep.
She walks—the lady of my delight—
  A shepherdess of sheep.

She holds her little thoughts in sight,
  Though gay they run and leap.

She is so circumspect and right
   She has her soul to keep.
She walks—the lady of my delight—
   A shepherdess of sheep.

Alice Meynell.

The Miller's Daughter ✍ ✍ ✍

IT is the miller's daughter,
   And she is grown so dear, so dear,
That I would be the jewel
   That trembles in her ear:
For hid in ringlets day and night,
I'd touch her neck so warm and bright.

And I would be the girdle
   About her dainty, dainty waist,
And her heart would beat against me,
   In sorrow and in rest:
And I should know if it beat right,
I'd clasp it round so close and tight.

And I would be the necklace,
   And all day long to fall and rise
Upon her balmy bosom,
   With her laughter or her sighs,
And I would lie so light, so light,
I scarce should be unclasp'd at night.

Alfred, Lord Tennyson.

71

A H ! don't tell o' mâidens; the oone var my bride
Is but little lik' too many mâidens bezide;
Not brāntèn, nar spitevul, nar wild;—she'v' a mind
Var to think what is right, an' a heart to be kind.

She's strâight an' she's slender, but not auver tal;
Her lims da move lightly, her veet be so smal:
A spirit o' heaven da breathe in her fiace,
An' a queen, to be stiately, must wā'ke wi' her piace.

Her frocks be so tidy, an' pirty, an' plâin:
She don't put on things that be fliarèn an' vain:
Her bonnet a-got but two ribbons, a-tied
Up under her chin, ar let down at the zide.

When she da speak to oone, she don't stiare an' grin;
There's sense in her looks vrom her eyes to her chin;
An' her vâice is so kind, var she's modest an' meek,
An' da look down to groun' a-beginnen to speak.

Her skin is so white as a lily, an' each
Ov her cheäks is so downy an' red as a peach:
She's pirty enough zittèn still; but my love
Da watch her to madness when oonce she da move.

An' when she da wā'ke huome vrom church, droo the
groun'
Wi' oone yarm in mine, an' wi' oone hangèn down,
I'm a-shiam'd o' myzuf; var I'm sure I must be
Oncommonly ugly along zide o' she.

Zoo don't ta'ke o''mâidens ; the oone var my bride
Is but little lik' too many mâidens bezide ;
Not brǎntèn, nar spitevul, nar wild ; she'v' a mind
Var to think what is right, an' a heart to be kind.

William Barnes.

Song

O SWEET delight, O more than human bliss,
　　With her to live that ever loving is !
To hear her speak whose words are so well placed
That she by them, as they in her are graced !
Those looks to view that feast the viewer's eye,
How blest is he that may so live and die !

Such love as this the Golden Times did know,
When all did reap, yet none took care to sow ;
Such love as this an endless summer makes,
And all distaste from frail affection takes.
So loved, so blest in my beloved am I :
Which till their eyes do ache, let iron men envý !

Thomas Campion.

A Match

I F love were what the rose is,
　　And I were like the leaf,
Our lives would grow together
In sad or singing weather,

Blown fields or flowerful closes,
 Green pleasure or grey grief;
If love were what the rose is,
 And I were like the leaf.

If I were what the words are,
 And love were like the tune,
With double sound and single
Delight our lips would mingle,
With kisses glad as birds are
 That get sweet rain at noon;
If I were what the words are
 And love were like the tune.

If you were life, my darling,
 And I your love were death,
We'd shine and snow together
Ere March made sweet the weather
With daffodil and starling
 And hours of fruitful breath;
If you were life, my darling,
 And I your love were death.

If you were thrall to sorrow,
 And I were page to joy,
We'd play for lives and seasons
With loving looks and treasons
And tears of night and morrow
 And laughs of maid and boy;
If you were thrall to sorrow,
 And I were page to joy.

If you were April's lady,
  And I were lord in May,
We'd throw with leaves for hours,
And draw for days with flowers,
Till day like night were shady
  And night were bright like day;
If you were April's lady,
  And I were lord in May.

If you were queen of pleasure
  And I were king of pain,
We'd hunt down love together,
Pluck out his flying-feather,
And teach his feet a measure,
  And find his mouth a rein!
If you were queen of pleasure,
  And I were king of pain.

                    Algernon Charles Swinburne.

Love's Garland

I WILL twine the white violet and I will twine the
    delicate narcissus with myrtle buds, and I will
twine laughing lilies, and I will twine the sweet crocus,
and I will twine therewithal the crimson hyacinth,
and I will twine lovers' roses, that on balsam-curled
Heliodora's temples my garland may shed its petals
over the lovelocks of her hair.

                    Meleager.
              (J. W. Mackail's translation.)

SHE walks in beauty, like the night
   Of cloudless climes and starry skies ;
And all that's best of dark and bright
   Meet in her aspect and her eyes :
Thus mellow'd to that tender light
   Which heaven to gaudy day denies.

One shade the more, one ray the less,
   Had half impair'd the nameless grace
Which waves in every raven tress,
   Or softly lightens o'er her face ;
Where thoughts serenely sweet express
   How pure, how dear their dwelling-place.

And on that cheek, and o'er that brow,
   So soft, so calm, yet eloquent,
The smiles that win, the tints that glow,
   But tell of days in goodness spent,
A mind at peace with all below,
   A heart whose love is innocent !

Lord Byron.

MY luve is like a red, red rose
   That's newly sprung in June :
My luve is like the melodie
   That's sweetly played in tune.

As fair thou art, my bonnie lass,
  So deep in luve am I :
And I will luve thee still, my dear,
  Till a' the seas gang dry.

Till a' the seas gang dry, my dear,
  And the rocks melt wi' the sun :
I will luve thee still, my dear,
  While the sands o' life shall run.

And fare thee weel, my only luve !
  And fare thee weel awhile !
And I will come again, my luve,
  Tho' it were ten thousand mile.

                              Robert Burns.

Song

S HE is not fair to outward view
    As many maidens be,
Her loveliness I never knew
    Until she smiled on me ;
Oh ! then I saw her eye was bright,
A well of love, a spring of light.

But now her looks are coy and cold,
  To mine they ne'er reply,
And yet I cease not to behold
  The love-light in her eye :
Her very frowns are fairer far
Than smiles of other maidens are.

                          Hartley Coleridge.

77

IT was not in the winter
　　Our loving lot was cast :
It was the time of roses,—
　　We plucked them as we passed !

That churlish season never frowned
　　On early lovers yet !
Oh no—the world was newly crowned
　　With flowers, when first we met.

'Twas twilight, and I bade you go,
　　But still you held me fast ;
It was the time of roses,—
　　We plucked them as we passed !

What else could peer my glowing cheek
　　That tears began to stud ?
And when I asked the like of Love
　　You snatched a damask bud,

And oped it to the dainty core
　　Still glowing to the last :
It was the time of roses,—
　　We plucked them as we passed !

Thomas Hood.

Song

G IVE a man a horse he can ride,
  Give a man a boat he can sail;
And his rank and wealth, his strength and health,
  On sea nor shore shall fail.

Give a man a pipe he can smoke,
  Give a man a book he can read;
And his home is bright with a calm delight,
  Though the room be poor indeed.

Give a man a girl he can love,
  As I, O my love, love thee;
And his heart is great with the pulse of Fate,
  At home, on land, on sea.

                              James Thomson.

The Message of the March Wind

(*Fragment*)

F AIR now is the springtide, now earth lies beholding
  With the eyes of a lover, the face of the sun;
Long lasteth the daylight, and hope is enfolding
  The green-growing acres with increase begun.

79

Now sweet, sweet it is through the land to be straying
   'Mid the birds and the blossoms and beasts of the
     field;
Love mingles with love, and no evil is weighing
   On thy heart or mine, where all sorrow is healed.

From township to township, o'er down and by tillage
   Fair, far have we wandered and long was the day;
But now cometh eve at the end of the village,
   Where over the grey wall the church riseth grey.

There is wind in the twilight; in the white road
     before us
   The straw from the ox-yard is blowing about;
The moon's rim is rising, a star glitters o'er us,
   And the vane on the spire-top is swinging in doubt.

Down there dips the highway, toward the bridge
     crossing over
   The brook that runs on to the Thames and the sea.
Draw closer, my sweet, we are lover and lover;
   This eve art thou given to gladness and me.

   .   .   .   .

Come back to the inn, love, and the lights and
     the fire,
   And the fiddler's old tune and the shuffling of feet;
For there in a while shall be rest and desire,
   And there shall the morrow's uprising be sweet.
                      William Morris.

I HAVE seen dawn and sunset on moors and
windy hills,
Coming in solemn beauty like slow old tunes of
Spain ;
I have seen the lady April bringing the daffodils,
Bringing the springing grass and the soft warm
April rain.

I have heard the song of the blossoms and the old
chant of the sea,
And seen strange lands from under the arched white
sails of ships ;
But the loveliest things of beauty **God** ever has showed
to me,
Are her voice, and her hair, and eyes, and the dear
red curve of her lips.

John Masefield.

The Passionate Shepherd to his Love

COME live with me and be my Love,
And we will all the pleasures prove
That hills and valleys, dale and field,
And all the craggy mountains yield.

F   81

There will we sit upon the rocks
And see the shepherds feed their flocks,
By shallow rivers, to whose falls
Melodious birds sing madrigals.

There will I make thee beds of roses
And a thousand fragrant posies,
A cap of flowers, and a kirtle
Embroider'd all with leaves of myrtle.

A gown made of the finest wool,
Which from our pretty lambs we pull,
Fair linéd slippers for the cold,
With buckles of the purest gold.

A belt of straw and ivy buds
With coral clasps and amber studs :
And if these pleasures may thee move,
Come live with me and be my Love.

Thy silver dishes for thy meat
As precious as the gods do eat,
Shall on an ivory table be
Prepared each day for thee and me.

The shepherd swains shall dance and sing
For thy delight each May-morning :
If these delights thy mind may move,
Then live with me and be my Love.

                              Christopher Marlowe.

Song

THERE is a garden in her face
    Where roses and white lilies blow ;
A heavenly paradise is that place,
    Wherein all pleasant fruits do grow ;
There cherries grow that none may buy,
Till Cherry-Ripe themselves do cry.

Those cherries fairly do enclose
    Of orient pearl a double row,
Which when her lovely laughter shows,
    They look like rose-buds fill'd with snow
Yet them no peer nor prince may buy,
Till Cherry-Ripe themselves do cry.

Her eyes like angels watch them still ;
    Her brows like bended bows do stand,
Threat'ning with piercing frowns to kill
    All that approach with eye or hand
These sacred cherries to come nigh,
—Till Cherry-Ripe themselves do cry !

Thomas Campion.

On his Mistress, the Queen of Bohemia

YOU meaner beauties of the night,
    That poorly satisfy our eyes
More by your number than your light,
    You common people of the skies ;
    What are you when the moon shall rise?

You curious chanters of the wood,
    That warble forth Dame Nature's lays,
Thinking your passions understood
    By your weak accents; what's your praise,
    When Philomel her voice shall raise?

You violets that first appear,
    By your pure purple mantles known
Like the proud virgins of the year,
    As if the spring were all your own;
    What are you when the rose is blown?

So, when my mistress shall be seen
    In form and beauty of her mind,
By virtue first, then choice, a Queen,
    Tell me if she were not designed
    The eclipse and glory of her kind?
                   Sir Henry Wotton.

Her Beauty

WHEN in the chronicle of wasted time
    I see descriptions of the fairest wights,
And beauty making beautiful old rhyme
In praise of ladies dead, and lovely knights;
Then in the blazon of sweet beauty's best
Of hand, of foot, of lip, of eye, of brow,
I see their antique pen would have exprest
Ev'n such a beauty as you master now.

So all their praises are but prophecies
Of this our time, all, you prefiguring ;
And for they look'd but with divining eyes,
They had not skill enough your worth to sing :
   For we, which now behold these present days,
    Have eyes to wonder, but lack tongues to praise.
               William Shakespeare.

Constancy

WERE I as base as is the lowly plain,
   And you, my Love, as high as heaven above,
Yet should the thoughts of me your humble swain
Ascend to heaven, in honour of my Love.

Were I as high as heaven above the plain,
And you, my Love, as humble and as low
As are the deepest bottoms of the main,
Whereso'er you were, with you my love should go.

Were you the earth, dear Love, and I the skies,
My love should shine on you like to the sun,
And look upon you with ten thousand eyes
Till heaven wax'd blind, and till the world were done.

Whereso'er I am, below, or else above you,
Whereso'er you are. my heart shall truly love you.
               John Sylvester.

SWEET is snow in summer for the thirsty to drink,
and sweet for sailors after winter to see the
garland of spring ; but most sweet when one cloak
shelters two lovers, and the tale of love is told by
both.

Asclepiades.
J. W. Mackail's translation.

SUN AND CLOUD, AND THE
WINDY HILLS

To see the sun to bed and to arise,
Like some hot amourist with glowing eyes,
Bursting the lazy bonds of sleep that bound him
With all his fires and travelling glories round him.

Charles Lamb.

To persons standing alone on a hill during a clear midnight such as this, the roll of the world eastward is almost a palpable movement. The sensation may be caused by the panoramic glide of the stars past earthly objects, which is perceptible in a few minutes of stillness, or by the better outlook upon space that a hill affords, or by the wind, or by the solitude; but whatever be its origin, the impression of riding along is vivid and abiding. The poetry of motion is a phrase much in use, and to enjoy the epic form of that gratification it is necessary to stand on a hill at a small hour of the night, and, having first expanded with a sense of difference from the mass of civilised mankind, who are dream-wrapt and disregardful of all such proceedings at this time, long and quietly watch your stately progress through the stars. After such a nocturnal reconnoitre it is hard to get back to earth, and to believe that the consciousness of such majestic speeding is derived from a tiny human frame.

Thomas Hardy (" *Far from the Madding Crowd* ").

The Sun

THE curious have an insufficient motive for going to the mountains if they do it to see the sunrise. The sun that leaps from a mountain peak is a sun past the dew of his birth; he has walked some way towards the common fires of noon. But on the flat country the uprising is early and fresh, the arc is wide, the career is long. The most distant clouds, converging in the beautiful and little-studied order of cloud perspective (for most painters treat clouds as though they formed perpendicular and not horizontal scenery), are those that gather at the central point of sunrise. On the plain, and there only, can the construction—but that is too little vital a word; I should rather say the organism — the unity, the design, of a sky be understood. The light wind that has been moving all night is seen to have not worked at random. It has shepherded some small flocks of cloud afield and folded others. There's husbandry in Heaven. And the order has, or seems to have, the sun for its midst. Not a line, not a curve, but confesses its membership in a design declared from horizon to horizon.

Alice Meynell.

Hymn of Apollo ∽ ∽ ∽ ∽ ∽

THE sleepless Hours who watch me as I lie,
    Curtained with star-inwoven tapestries,
From the broad moonlight of the sky,
    Fanning the busy dreams from my dim eyes,
Waken me when their Mother, the grey Dawn,
Tells them that dreams and that the moon is gone.

Then I arise, and, climbing Heaven's blue dome,
    I walk over the mountains and the waves,
Leaving my robe upon the ocean foam ;
    My footsteps pave the clouds with fire ; the caves
Are filled with my bright presence, and the air
Leaves the green Earth to my embraces bare.

The sunbeams are my shafts, with which I kill
    Deceit, that loves the night and fears the day ;
All men who do or even imagine ill
    Fly me, and from the glory of my ray
Good minds and open actions take new might,
Until diminished by the reign of Night.

I feed the clouds, the rainbows, and the flowers,
    With their ethereal colours ; the Moon's globe,
And the pure stars in their eternal bowers,
    Are cinctured with my power as with a robe ;
Whatever lamps on Earth or Heaven may shine
Are portions of one power, which is mine.

I stand at noon upon the peak of Heaven;
    Then with unwilling steps I wander down
Into the clouds of the Atlantic even;
    For grief that I depart they weep and frown:
What look is more delightful than the smile
With which I soothe them from the western isle?

I am the eye with which the Universe
    Beholds itself, and knows itself divine;
All harmony of instrument or verse,
    All prophecy, all medicine, are mine,
All light of art or nature;—to my song
Victory and praise in their own right belong.

                    Percy Bysshe Shelley.

Youth at the Summit

I GOT up the mountain edge, and from the top saw
the world stretch out—cornlands and forest, the
river winding among meadow-flats, and right off, like
a hem of the sky, the moving sea, with snatches of
foam, and large ships reaching forward, out-bound.
And then I thought no more, but my heart leapt to
meet the wind, and I ran, and I ran. I felt my legs
under me, I felt the wind buffet me, hit me on the
cheek; the sun shone, the bees swept past me singing; and I too sang, shouted, World, world, I am
coming!

                    Maurice Hewlett.
            (Pan and the Young Shepherd.)

Morning on Etna ✧ ✧ ✧ ✧ ✧

THE mules, I think, will not be here this hour.
    They feel the cool wet turf under their feet
By the stream-side, after the dusty lanes
In which they have toil'd all night from Catana,
And scarcely will they budge a yard.   O Pan,
How gracious is the mountain at this hour!
A thousand times have I been here alone,
Or with the revellers from the mountain towns,
But never on so fair a morn ;—the sun
Is shining on the brilliant mountain crests,
And on the highest pines ; but further down
Here in the valley is in shade ; the sward
Is dark, and on the stream the mist still hangs ;
One sees one's footprints crush'd in the wet grass,
One's breath curls in the air ; and on these pines
That climb from the stream's edge, the long grey
        tufts,
Which the goats love, are jewell'd thick with dew.

                                    Matthew Arnold.

The Horizon ✧ ✧ ✧ ✧ ✧

TO mount a hill is to lift with you something lighter
    and brighter than yourself or than any meaner
burden. You lift the world, you raise the horizon ;
you give a signal for the distance to stand up. It is

like the scene in the Vatican when a Cardinal, with his dramatic Italian hands, bids the kneeling groups to arise. He does more than bid them. He lifts them, he gathers them up, far and near, with the upward gesture of both arms ; he takes them to their feet with the compulsion of his expressive force. Or it is as when a conductor takes his players to successive heights of music. You summon the sea, you bring the mountains, the distances unfold unlooked-for wings and take an even flight. You are but a man lifting his weight upon the upward road, but as you climb the circle of the world goes up to face you. . . . It is the law whereby the eye and the horizon answer one another that makes the way up a hill so full of universal movement. All the landscape is on pilgrimage. The town gathers itself closer, and its inner harbours literally come to light ; the headlands repeat themselves ; little cups within the treeless hills open and show their farms. In the sea are many regions. A breeze is at play for a mile or two, and the surface is turned. There are roads and curves in the blue and in the white. Not a step of your journey up the height that has not its replies in the steady motion of land and sea. Things rise together like a flock of many-feathered birds.

Alice Meynell.

MOVING up the sweet short turf, at every step my heart seemed to obtain a wider horizon of feeling ; with every inhalation of rich pure air, a deeper desire. The very light of the sun was whiter and more brilliant here. By the time I had reached the summit I had entirely forgotten the petty circumstances and the annoyances of existence. I felt myself, myself. There was an intrenchment on the summit, and going down into the fosse I walked round it slowly to recover breath. On the southwestern side there was a spot where the outer bank had partially slipped, leaving a gap. There the view was over a broad plain, beautiful with wheat, and inclosed by a perfect amphitheatre of green hills. Through these hills there was one narrow groove, or pass, southwards, where the white clouds seemed to close in the horizon. Woods hid the scattered hamlets and farmhouses, so that I was quite alone.

I was utterly alone with the sun and the earth. Lying down on the grass, I spoke in my soul to the earth, the sun, the air, and the distant sea far beyond sight. I thought of the earth's firmness—I felt it bear me up ; through the grassy couch there came an influence as if I could feel the great earth speaking to me. I thought of the wandering air—its pureness, which is its beauty ; the air touched me and gave me something of itself. I spoke to the sea : though so far, in my mind I saw it, green at the rim of the earth and blue in deeper ocean ; I desired to have its strength, its mystery and glory. Then I addressed the sun, desiring the soul equivalent of his light and brilliance, his endurance and unwearied race. I turned to the blue heaven over, gazing into its depth, inhaling its exquisite colour and sweetness. The rich blue of the unattainable flower of the sky drew my soul towards it, and there it rested, for pure colour is rest of heart. By all these I prayed ; I felt an emotion of the soul beyond all definition ; prayer is a puny thing to it, and the word is a rude sign to the feeling, but I know no other.

By the blue heaven, by the rolling sun bursting through untrodden space, a new ocean of ether every day unveiled. By the fresh and wandering air encompassing the world ; by the sea sounding on the shore—the green sea white-flecked at the margin and the deep ocean ; by the strong earth under me. Then, returning, I prayed by the sweet thyme, whose little flowers I touched with my hand ; by the slender grass ; by the crumble of dry chalky earth I took up and let fall through my fingers. Touching the crumble of earth, the blade of grass, the thyme flower, breathing the earth-encircling air, thinking of the sea and the sky, holding out my hand for the sunbeams to touch it, prone on the sward in token of deep reverence, thus I prayed that I might touch to the unutterable existence infinitely higher than deity.

Richard Jefferies.

COME down, O maid, from yonder mountain height:
What pleasure lives in height (the shepherd sang)
In height and cold, the splendour of the hills?
But cease to move so near the Heavens, and cease
To glide a sunbeam by the blasted Pine,
To sit a star upon the sparkling spire;
And come, for Love is of the valley, come,
For Love is of the valley, come thou down
And find him; by the happy threshold, he,
Or hand in hand with Plenty in the maize,
Or red with spirted purple of the vats,
Or foxlike in the vine; nor cares to walk
With Death and Morning on the silver horns,
Nor wilt thou snare him in the white ravine,
Nor find him dropt upon the firths of ice,
That huddling slant in furrow-cloven falls
To roll the torrent out of dusky doors:
But follow; let the torrent dance thee down
To find him in the valley; let the wild
Lean-headed Eagles yelp alone, and leave
The monstrous ledges there to slope, and spill
Their thousand wreaths of dangling water-smoke,
That like a broken purpose waste in air:
So waste not thou; but come; for all the vales
Await thee; azure pillars of the hearth
Arise to thee; the children call, and I
Thy shepherd pipe, and sweet is every sound,
Sweeter thy voice, but every sound is sweet;

Myriads of rivulets hurrying thro' the lawn,
The moan of doves in immemorial elms,
And murmuring of innumerable bees.

Alfred, Lord Tennyson.

Knowledge ᗧ ᗧ ᗧ ᗧ ᗧ

M EN say they know many things ;
But lo ! they have taken wings,—
The arts and sciences,
And a thousand appliances ;
The wind that blows
Is all that anybody knows.

H. D. Thoreau.

The South-West Wind ᗧ ᗧ ᗧ ᗧ

T HE most certain and most conquering of all is
the south-west wind. You do not look to the
weather-vane to decide what shall be the style of your
greeting to his morning. There is no arbitrary rule of
courtesy between you and him, and you need no arrow
to point to his distinctions, and to indicate to you the
right manner of treating such a visitant.

He prepares the dawn. While it is still dark the
air is warned of his presence, and before the window

was opened he was already in the room. His sun—for the sun is his—rises in the south-west mood, with a bloom on the blue, the grey, or the gold. When the south-west is cold, the cold is his own cold—round, blunt, full, and gradual in its very strength. It is a fresh cold, that comes with an approach, and does not challenge you in the manner of an unauthorised stranger, but instantly gets your leave, and even a welcome to your house of life. He follows your breath in at your throat, and your eyes are open to let him in, even when he is cold. Your blood cools, but does not hide from him.

He has a splendid way with his sky. In his flight, which is that, not of a bird, but of a flock of birds, he flies high and low at once: high with his higher clouds, that keep long in the sight of man, seeming to move slowly; and low with the coloured clouds that breast the hills and are near to tree-tops. These the south-west wind tosses up from his soft horizon, round and successive. They are tinted somewhat like ripe clover-fields, or like hay-fields just before the cutting, when all the grass is in flower, and they are, oftener than all other clouds, in shadow. These low-lying flocks are swift and brief; the wind casts them before him, from the western verge to the eastern.

Alice Meynell.

Ode to the West Wind ❧ ❧ ❧ ❧

O WILD West Wind, thou breath of Autumn's
    being,
Thou from whose unseen presence the leaves dead
Are driven like ghosts from an enchanter fleeing,

    Yellow, and black, and pale, and hectic red,
Pestilence-stricken multitudes !   O thou
    Who chariotest to their dark wintry bed

The wingèd seeds, where they lie cold and low,
    Each like a corpse within its grave, until
Thine azure sister of the Spring shall blow

    Her clarion o'er the dreaming earth, and fill
(Driving sweet buds like flocks to feed in air)
    With living hues and odours plain and hill ;

Wild Spirit which art moving everywhere ;
Destroyer and preserver ; hear, oh hear !

Thou on whose stream, 'mid the steep sky's commotion,
    Loose clouds like earth's decaying leaves are shed,
Shook from the tangled boughs of heaven and ocean,

    Angels of rain and lightning ! there are spread
On the blue surface of thine airy surge,
    Like the bright hair uplifted from the head

Of some fierce Mænad, even from the dim verge
    Of the horizon to the zenith's height,
The locks of the approaching storm.   Thou dirge

    Of the dying year, to which this closing night
Will be the dome of a vast sepulchre,
    Vaulted with all thy congregated might

Of vapours, from whose solid atmosphere
Black rain, and fire, and hail, will burst : Oh hear !

Thou who didst waken from his summer dreams
   The blue Mediterranean, where he lay,
Lulled by the coil of his crystalline streams,
   Beside a pumice isle in Baiæ's bay,
And saw in sleep old palaces and towers
   Quivering within the wave's intenser day,
All overgrown with azure moss, and flowers
   So sweet the sense faints picturing them !   Thou
For whose path the Atlantic's level powers
   Cleave themselves into chasms, while far below
The sea-blooms and the oozy woods which wear
   The sapless foliage of the ocean know
Thy voice, and suddenly grow grey with fear,
And tremble and despoil themselves : Oh, hear !

If I were a dead leaf thou mightest bear ;
   If I were a swift cloud to fly with thee ;
A wave to pant beneath thy power, and share
   The impulse of thy strength, only less free
Than thou, O uncontrollable ! if even
   I were as in my boyhood, and could be
The comrade of thy wanderings over heaven,
   As then, when to outstrip thy skiey speed
Scarce seemed a vision,—I would ne'er have striven
   As thus with thee in prayer in my sore need.
Oh lift me as a wave, a leaf, a cloud !
   I fall upon the thorns of life ! I bleed !

A heavy weight of hours has chained and bowed
One too like thee—tameless, and swift, and proud.

Make me thy lyre, even as the forest is :
    What if my leaves are falling like its own ?
The tumult of thy mighty harmonies
    Will take from both a deep autumnal tone,
Sweet though in sadness.   Be thou, Spirit fierce,
    My spirit !   Be thou me, impetuous one !
Drive my dead thoughts over the universe,
    Like withered leaves, to quicken a new birth ;
And, by the incantation of this verse,
    Scatter, as from an unextinguished hearth
Ashes and sparks, my words among mankind !
    Be through my lips to unawakened earth
The trumpet of a prophecy !   O Wind,
If Winter comes, can Spring be far behind ?

                              Percy Bysshe Shelley.

Curious Observations about the Weather ∽　　∽

(Not only to know it for a month, but for ever ; by one that
    stiles himself Erra Pater)

To know the Weather by the rising and setting of the Sun.

IF the sun rise red and fiery, expect wind and rain.
    If at sun-rising it be cloudy, and the clouds
    vanish away as the sun riseth higher, it is a sure
    sign of fair weather.

Likewise, if the sun setteth red, it is a sign of fair weather. If it set in a muddy misty colour, it is a sign of rain.

To know the Weather by the Moon.

If the Moon shines clear, and not compassed about with Mist, it will be fair weather.

If the Moon be compassed about with a circle, like a great wheel, or is misty and dim, wind or rain follows, or snow within twenty-four hours.

To know the Weather by the Stars.

The stars more bright than ordinary in summer, signifies great winds and wet.

If they twinkle or blaze in winter, the wind north or east, is a sign of great frost. When they are seen to fall or shoot, is a sign of great rain and winds.

To know the Weather by the Clouds.

If they are round, and of a dapple grey colour, and the wind north or east, fair weather for two or three days after.

If the clouds appear like towers or rocks, signify great showers.

If clouds that are small grow bigger and bigger, it is a sign of much rain. But if great clouds waste and grow less, it is a sign of fair weather.

Of the Winds.

If in spring there be north and east winds, and great
draughts, so will the summer quarter be, and consequently, scarcity of grass and hay.   So the
contrary, will be plenteous of grass and hay ; for
there is as much south and west wind, as north
and east too, and consequently as many wet years
as dry.

Old Book.

Rain

IT ain't no use to grumble and complain ;
    It's jest as cheap and easy to rejoice ;
When God sorts out the weather and sends rain,
    W'y, rain's my choice.

James Whitcomb Riley.

Morning

O WHITE wind of the dawn,
    The path that you have trod
From night to day is drawn,
    From godhead unto God !

Your face is made aware
    Of ardour and surprise ;
The stars are in your hair,
    The Sun is in your eyes.

103

And all my blood is stung
   To follow and to find
Another world as young
   As you are, and as kind.

Ah me, how more than sweet
   To shake off weight of ills,
And follow where your feet
   Have danced upon the hills !

Gerald Gould.

Clouds 〜 〜 〜 〜 〜 〜

THE cloud, moreover, controls the sun, not merely by keeping the custody of his rays, but by becoming the counsellor of his temper. The cloud veils an angry sun, or, more terribly, lets fly an angry ray, suddenly bright upon tree and tower, with iron-grey storm for a background. Or when anger had but threatened, the cloud reveals him, gentle beyond hope. It makes peace, constantly, just before sunset.

It is in the confidence of the winds, and wears their colours. There is a heavenly game, on south-west wind days, when the clouds are bowled by a breeze from behind the evening. They are round and brilliant, and come leaping up from the horizon for hours. This is a frolic and haphazard sky.

All unlike this is the sky that has a centre, and **stands** composed about it. As the clouds marshalled the earthly mountains, so the clouds in turn are now ranged. The tops of all the celestial Andes aloft are swept at once by a single ray, warmed with a single colour. Promontory after league-long promontory of a stiller Mediterranean in the sky is called out of mist and grey by the same finger. The cloudland is very great, but a sunbeam makes all its nations and continents sudden with light.

Alice Meynell.

The Cloud

I BRING fresh showers for the thirsting flowers
    From the seas and the streams;
I bear light shade for the leaves when laid
    In their noonday dreams.
From my wings are shaken the dews that waken
    The sweet buds every one,
When rocked to rest on their Mother's breast,
    As she dances about the sun.
I wield the flail of the lashing hail,
    And whiten the green plains under;
And then again I dissolve it in rain,
    And laugh as I pass in thunder.

I sift the snow on the mountains below,
    And their great pines groan aghast;
And all the night 'tis my pillow white,
    While I sleep in the arms of the Blast.

Sublime on the towers of my skiey bowers
    Lightning my pilot sits;
In a cavern under is fettered the Thunder,
    It struggles and howls at fits.
Over earth and ocean with gentle motion
    This pilot is guiding me,
Lured by the love of the Genii that move
    In the depths of the purple sea;
Over the rills and the crags and the hills,
    Over the lakes and the plains,
Wherever he dream under mountain or stream
    The Spirit he loves remains;
And I all the while bask in heaven's blue smile,
    Whilst he is dissolving in rains.

The sanguine Sunrise, with his meteor eyes,
    And his burning plumes outspread,
Leaps on the back of my sailing rack,
    When the morning star shines dead:
As on the jag of a mountain-crag
    Which an earthquake rocks and swings
An eagle alit one moment may sit
    In the light of its golden wings.
And, when Sunset may breathe, from the lit sea
        beneath,
    Its ardours of rest and of love,
And the crimson pall of eve may fall
    From the depth of heaven above,
With wings folded I rest on mine airy nest,
    As still as a brooding dove.

That orbèd maiden with white fire laden
    Whom mortals call the Moon
Glides glimmering o'er my fleece-like floor
    By the midnight breezes strewn ;
And wherever the beat of her unseen feet,
    Which only the angels hear,
May have broken the woof of my tent's thin roof,
    The Stars peep behind her and peer.
And I laugh to see them whirl and flee
    Like a swarm of golden bees,
When I widen the rent in my wind-built tent,—
    Till the calm rivers, lakes, and seas,
Like strips of the sky fallen through me on high,
    Are each paved with the moon and these.

I bind the Sun's throne with a burning zone,
    And the Moon's with a girdle of pearl ;
The volcanoes are dim, and the Stars reel and swim,
    When the Whirlwinds my banner unfurl.
From cape to cape, with a bridge-like shape,
    Over a torrent sea,
Sunbeam-proof, I hang like a roof ;
    The mountains its columns be.
The triumphal arch through which I march,
    With hurricane, fire, and snow,
When the Powers of the air are chained to my
      chair ;
    Is the million-coloured bow ;
The Sphere-fire above its soft colours wove,
    While the moist Earth was laughing below.

I am the daughter of Earth and Water,
  And the nursling of the Sky:
I pass through the pores of the ocean and shores;
  I change, but I cannot die.
For after the rain, when with never a stain
  The pavilion of heaven is bare,
And the winds, and sunbeams with their convex gleams
  Build up the blue dome of air,
I silently laugh at my own cenotaph,—
  And out of the caverns of rain,
Like a child from the womb, like a ghost from the
    tomb,
  I arise, and unbuild it again.

                              Percy Bysshe Shelley.

Sussex   ∽   ∽   ∽   ∽

GOD gave all men all earth to love,
    But since our hearts are small,
Ordained for each one spot should prove
    Beloved over all;
That as He watched Creation's birth,
    So we, in godlike mood,
May of our love create our earth
    And see that it is good.

So one shall Baltic pines content,
    As one some Surrey glade,
Or one the palm-grove's droned lament
    Before Levuka's trade.

Each to his choice, and I rejoice
    The lot has fallen to me
In a fair ground—in a fair ground—
    Yea, Sussex by the sea !

No tender-hearted garden crowns,
    No bosomed woods adorn
Our blunt, bow-headed, whale-backed Downs,
    But gnarled and writhen thorn—
Bare slopes where chasing shadows skim.
    And through the gaps revealed
Belt upon belt, the wooded, dim
    Blue goodness of the Weald.

Clean of officious fence or hedge,
    Half-wild and wholly tame,
The wise turf cloaks the white cliff edge
    As when the Romans came.
What sign of those that fought and died
    At shift of sword and sword ?
The barrow and the camp abide,
    The sunlight and the sward.

Here leaps ashore the full Sou' west
    All heavy-winged with brine,
Here lies above the golden crest
    The Channel's leaden line ;
And here the sea-fogs lap and cling,
    And here, each warning each,
The sheep-bells and the ship-bells ring
    Along the hidden beach.

We have no waters to delight
    Our broad and brookless vales—
Only the dewpond on the height
    Unfed, that never fails,
Whereby no tattered herbage tells
    Which way the season flies—
Only our close-bit thyme that smells
    Like dawn in Paradise.

Here through the strong unhampered days
    The tinkling silence thrills ;
Or little, lost, Down churches praise
    The Lord who made the hills :
But here the Old Gods guard their round,
    And, in her secret heart,
The heathen kingdom Wilfrid found
    Dreams, as she dwells, apart.

Though all the rest were all my share,
    With equal soul I'd see
Her nine-and-thirty sisters fair,
    Yet none more fair than she.
Choose ye your need from Thames to Tweed,
    And I will choose instead
Such lands as lie 'twixt Rake and Rye,
    Black Down and Beachy Head.

I will go out against the sun
    Where the rolled scarp retires,
And the Long Man of Wilmington
    Looks naked towards the shires ;

And east till doubling Rother crawls
    To find the fickle tide,
By dry and sea-forgotten walls,
    Our ports of stranded pride.

I will go north about the shaws
    And the deep ghylls that breed
Huge oaks and old, the which we hold
    No more than "Sussex weed";
Or south where windy Piddinghoe's
    Begilded dolphin veers,
And black beside wide-bankèd Ouse ·
    Lie down our Sussex steers.

So to the land our hearts we give
    Till the sure magic strike,
And Memory, Use, and Love make live
    Us and our fields alike—
That deeper than our speech and thought
    Beyond our reason's sway,
Clay of the pit whence we were wrought
    Yearns to its fellow-clay.

God gives all men all earth to love,
    But since man's heart is small,
Ordains for each one spot shall prove
    Beloved over all.
Each to his choice, and I rejoice
    The lot has fallen to me
In a fair ground—in a fair ground—
    Yea, Sussex by the sea!
                        Rudyard Kipling.

O BOLD majestic downs, smooth, fair and lonely ;
    O still solitude, only matched in the skies ;
        Perilous in steep places,
        Soft in the level races,
Where sweeping in phantom silence the cloudland
    flies ;
With lovely undulation of fall and rise ;
        Entrenched with thickets thorned,
By delicate miniature dainty flowers adorned !

I climb your crown, and lo ! a sight surprising
Of sea in front uprising, steep and wide :
        And scattered ships ascending
        To heaven, lost in the blending
Of distant blues, where water and sky divide,
Urging their engines against wind and tide,
        And all so small and slow
They seem to be wearily pointing the way they would
    go.

The accumulated murmur of soft plashing,
Of waves on rocks dashing, and searching the sands ;
        Takes my ear, in the veering
        Baffled wind, as rearing
Upright at the cliff, to the gullies and rifts he stands ;
And his conquering surges scour out over the lands ;
        While again at the foot of the downs
He masses his strength to recover the topmost crowns.

                                    Robert Bridges.

WHEN I am living in the Midlands
        That are sodden and unkind,
I light my lamp in the evening :
    My work is left behind ;
And the great hills of the South Country
    Come back into my mind.

The great hills of the South Country
    They stand along the sea :
And it's there walking in the high woods
    That I could wish to be,
And the men that were boys when I was a boy
    Walking along with me.

The men that live in North England
    I saw them for a day :
Their hearts are set upon the waste fells,
    Their skies are fast and grey :
From their castle-walls a man may see
    The mountains far away.

The men that live in West England
    They see the Severn strong,
A-rolling on rough water brown
    Light aspen leaves along.
They have the secret of the Rocks,
    And the oldest kind of song.

But the men that live in the South Country
  Are the kindest and most wise,
They get their laughter from the loud surf
  And the faith in their happy eyes
Comes surely from our Sister the Spring
  When over the sea she flies ;
The violets suddenly bloom at her feet,
  She blesses us with surprise.

I never get between the pines
  But I smell the Sussex air,
Nor I never come on a belt of sand
  But the old place is there.
And along the sky the line of the downs
  So noble and so bare.

A lost thing could I never find,
  Nor a broken thing mend :
And I fear I shall be all alone
  When I get towards the end.
Who will there be to comfort me
  Or who will be my friend ?

I will gather and carefully make my friends
  Of the men of the Sussex Weald.
They watch the stars from silent folds,
  They stiffly plough the field.
By them and the God of the South Country
  My poor soul shall be healed.

If I ever become a rich man,
  Or if ever I grow to be old,
I will build a house with deep thatch
  To shelter me from the cold,
And there shall the Sussex songs be sung
  And the story of Sussex told.

I will hold my house in the high wood
  Within a walk of the sea,
And the men that were boys when I was a boy
  Shall sit and drink with me.

Hilaire Belloc.

Hill Aspirations

ODDLY enough, that desire which we all have at times for wings, or at all events for the power of flight, and which, like other vague and idle promptings, is capable of cultivation and of being made a real source of pleasure, most often comes to me on these great green hills. Here are no inviting woods and mysterious green shades that ask to be explored: they stand naked to the sky, and on them the mind becomes more aërial, less conscious of gravity and a too solid body. Standing on one great green hill, and looking across vast intervening hollows to other round heights and hills beyond and far away, the wish is more than a wish, and I can almost realise the sensation of being other than I am—a creature

with the instinct of flight and the correlated faculty ;
that in a little while, when I have gazed my full and
am ready to change my place, I shall lift great heron-
like wings and fly with little effort to other points of
view.

W. H. Hudson.

COMPANIONS

A West-Country squire on his death-bed was visited by the parson.

"You are going to a better world," said the Parson.

"I don't want no better world. With my white-vaced mare and a thousand a year I don't want no better world. Her'd go over gates one arter t'other—tip—tip—tip."

Cornish Magazine.

Two Epitaphs from the Greek Anthology

I. On a Maltese Watch-Dog.

HERE the stone says it holds the white dog from
Melita, the most faithful guardian of Eumelus;
Bull they called him while he was yet alive; but now
his voice is prisoned in the silent pathways of night.

Tymnes.

II. On a Favourite Dog.

THOU who passest on the path, if haply thou dost
mark this monument, laugh not, I pray thee,
though it is a dog's grave; tears fell for me, and the
dust was heaped above me by a master's hands, who
likewise engraved these words on my tomb.

Author unknown.
(J. W. Mackail's translation.)

To Rufus, A Spaniel

RUFUS, a bright New Year! A savoury stew,
Bones, broth and biscuits, is prepared for you.
See how it steams in your enamelled dish,
Mixed in each part according to your wish.

Hide in your straw the bones you cannot crunch—
They'll come in handy for to-morrow's lunch;
Abstract with care each tasty scrap of meat,
Remove each biscuit to a fresh retreat
(A dog, I judge, would deem himself disgraced
Who ate a biscuit where he found it placed);
Then nuzzle round and make your final sweep,
And sleep, replete, your after-dinner sleep.
High in our hall we've piled the fire with logs
For you, the *doyen* of our corps of dogs.
There, when the stroll that health demands is done,
Your right to ease by due exertion won,
There shall you come, and on your long-haired mat,
Thrice turning round, shall tread the jungle flat,
And, rhythmically snoring, dream away
The peaceful evening of your New Year's day.

Rufus! there are who hesitate to own
Merits, they say, your master sees alone.
They judge you stupid, for you show no bent
To any poodle-dog accomplishment.
Your stubborn nature never stooped to learn
Tricks by which mumming dogs their biscuits earn.
Men mostly find you, if they change their seat,
Couchant obnoxious to their blundering feet;
Then, when a door is closed, you steadily
Misjudge the side on which you ought to be;
Yelping outside when all your friends are in,
You raise the echoes with your ceaseless din,
Or, always wrong, but turn and turn about,

Howling inside when all the world is out.
They scorn your gestures and interpret ill
Your humble signs of friendship and goodwill.
Laugh at your gambols, and pursue with jeers
The ringlets clustered on your spreading ears ;
See without sympathy your sore distress
When Ray obtains the coveted caress,
And you, a jealous lump of growl and glare,
Hide from the world your head beneath a chair.
They say your legs are bandy—so they are :
Nature so formed them that they might go far ;
They cannot brook your music ; they assail
The joyful quiverings of your stumpy tail—
In short, in one anathema confound
Shape, mind and heart, and all my little hound.
Well, let them rail.   If, since your life began,
Beyond the customary lot of man
Staunchness was yours ; if of your faithful heart
Malice and scorn could never claim a part ;
If in your master, loving while you live,
You own no fault or own it to forgive ;
If, as you lay your head upon his knee,
Your deep-drawn sighs proclaim your sympathy ;
If faith and friendship, growing with your age,
Speak through your eyes and all his love engage ;
If by that master's wish your life you rule—
If this be folly, Rufus, you're a fool.

Old dog, content you ; Rufus, have no fear :
While life is yours and mine your place is here.

And when the day shall come, as come it must,
When Rufus goes to mingle with the dust
(If Fate ordains that you shall pass before
To the abhorred and sunless Stygian shore),
I think old Charon, punting through the dark,
Will hear a sudden friendly little bark ;
And on the shore he'll mark without a frown
A flap-eared doggie, bandy-legged and brown.
He'll take you in : since watermen are kind,
He'd scorn to leave my little dog behind.
He'll ask no obol, but instal you there
On Styx's further bank without a fare.
There shall you sniff his cargoes as they come,
And droop your head, and turn, and still be dumb—
Till one fine day, half joyful, half in fear,
You run and prick a recognising ear,
And last, oh, rapture ! leaping to his hand,
Salute your master as he steps to land.

R. C. Lehmann.

Dick ∽ ∽ ∽ ∽ ∽ ∽

DICK still lives, and long may he live ! As he was
never born, possibly he may never die ; be it
so, he will miss us when we are gone. I could say
much of him, but agree with the lively and admirable
Dr. Jortin, when, in his dedication of his *Remarks on
Ecclesiastical History* to the then (1752) Archbishop

of Canterbury, he excuses himself for not following the modern custom of praising his Patron, by reminding his Grace "that it was a custom amongst the ancients, *not to sacrifice to heroes till after sunset.*" I defer my sacrifice till Dick's sun is set.

I think every family should have a dog : it is like having a perpetual baby ; it is the plaything and crony of the whole house. It keeps them all young. All unite upon Dick. And then he tells no tales, betrays no secrets, never sulks, asks no troublesome questions, never gets into debt, never coming down late for breakfast, or coming in by his Chubb *too early* to bed—is always ready for a bit of fun, lies in wait for it, and you may, if choleric, to your relief, kick him instead of someone else, who would not take it so meekly, and, moreover, would certainly not, as he does, ask your pardon for being kicked.

Never put a collar on your dog—it only gets him stolen ; give him only one meal a day, and let that, as Dame Dorothy, Sir Thomas Browne's wife, would say, be "rayther under." Wash him once a week, and always wash the soap out ; and let him be carefully combed and brushed twice a week.

By the bye, I was wrong in saying that it was Burns who said Man is the God of the Dog—he got it from Bacon's *Essay on Atheism*.

Dr. John Brown.

I'LL sing you a song, and a merry, merry song,
　Concerning our Yorkshire Jen ;
Who never yet ran with horse or mare,
　That ever she cared for a pin.

When first she came to Newmarket town
　The sportsmen all view'd her around ;
All the cry was, "Alas, poor wench,
　Thou never can run this ground ! "

When they came to the starting-post,
　The Mare look'd very smart ;
And let them all say what they will,
　She never lost her start.

When they got to the two-mile post,
　Poor Jenny was cast behind :
She was cast behind, she was cast behind,
　All for to take her wind.

When they got to the three-mile post,
　The Mare look'd very pale—
SHE LAID DOWN HER EARS ON HER BONNY NECK,
　AND BY THEM ALL DID SHE SAIL ;

"Come follow me, come follow me,
　All you that run so neat ;
And ere that you catch me again,
　I'll make you all to sweat."

When she got to the winning-post,
    The people all gave a shout ;
And Jenny click'd up her lily-white foot,
    And jumped like any buck.

The Jockey said to her, " This race you have run,
    This race for me you have got ;
You could gallop it all over again,
    When the rest could hardly trot ! "

(From *Euphranor.*)

The Irish Cob

OH, that ride ! that first ride !—most truly it was
an epoch in my existence ; and I still look
back to it with feelings of longing and regret. People
may talk of first love—it is a very agreeable event,
I dare say—but give me the flush, and triumph, and
glorious sweat of a first ride, like mine on the mighty
cob ! My whole frame was shaken, it is true ; and
during one long week I could hardly move foot or
hand ; but what of that ? By that one trial I had
become free, as I may say, of the whole equine species.
No more fatigue, no more stiffness of joints, after
that first ride round the Devil's Hill on the cob. Oh,
that cob ! that Irish cob !—may the sod lie lightly
over the bones of the strongest, speediest, and most
gallant of its kind !

It was thus that the passion for the equine race
was first awakened within me—a passion which, up

to the present time, has been rather on the increase than diminishing. It is no blind passion; the horse being a noble and generous creature, intended by the All-Wise to be the helper and friend of man, to whom he stands next in the order of creation.

George Borrow.

BIRDS, BLOSSOMS, AND TREES

God's jocund lyttel fowles.

Old Writer.

The trees and the flowers
    Shall now be my Friend:
The trees and the flowers
    That never pretend.
They keep to their nature
    As, quiet and true,
They grow to their stature
    And bloom in their hue.

Mary F. Robinson.

The holes were already dug, and they set to work. Winterborne's fingers were endowed with a gentle conjurer's touch in spreading the roots of each little tree, resulting in a sort of caress under which the delicate fibres all laid themselves out in their proper directions for growth. He put most of these roots towards the south-west; for, he said, in forty years' time, when some great gale is blowing from that quarter, the trees will require the strongest holdfast on that side to stand against it and not fall.

"How they sigh directly we put 'em upright, though while they are lying down they don't sigh at all," said Marty.

"Do they?" said Giles. "I've never noticed it."

She erected one of the young pines into its hole, and held up her finger; the soft musical breathing instantly set in, which was not to cease night or day till the grown tree should be felled—probably long after the two planters should be felled themselves.

Thomas Hardy ("*The Woodlanders*").

Who does his duty is a question
    Too complex to be solved by me,
But he, I venture the suggestion,
    Does part of his that plants a tree.

J. R. Lowell.

The Very Birds of the Air ∽   ∽   ∽   ∽

NAY more, the very birds of the air, those that be not hawks, are both so many and so useful and pleasant to mankind, that I must not let them pass without some observations. They both feed and refresh him—feed him with their choice bodies, and refresh him with their heavenly voices. I will not undertake to mention the several kinds of fowl by which this is done, and his curious palate pleased by day, and which with their very excrements afford him a soft lodging at night—these I will pass by; but not those little nimble musicians of the air, that warble forth their curious ditties, with which nature hath furnished them to the shame of art.

As first the lark, when she means to rejoice, to cheer herself and those that hear her; she then quits the earth, and sings as she ascends higher into the air, and having ended her heavenly employment, grows then mute and sad, to think she must descend to the dull earth, which she would not touch, but for necessity.

How do the blackbird and thrassel with their melodious voices bid welcome to the cheerful spring, as in their fixed months warble forth such ditties as no art or instrument can reach to !

Nay, the smaller birds also do the like in their particular seasons, as namely the leverock, the titlark, the little linnet, and the honest robin, that loves mankind both alive and dead.

But the nightingale, another of my airy creatures, breathes such sweet loud music out of her little instrumental throat, that it might make mankind to think miracles are not ceased. He that at midnight, when the very labourer sleeps securely, should hear, as I have very often, the clear airs, the sweet descants, the natural rising and falling, the doubling and re-doubling of her voice, might well be lifted above earth, and say, " Lord, what music hast Thou provided for the saints in heaven, when Thou affordest bad men such music on earth ? "

Izaak Walton.

The Blackbird ∽ ∽ ∽ ∽ ∽

O V al the birds upon the wing
　　Between the zunny show'rs o' spring,
Var al the lark, a-swingèn high,
Mid zing sweet ditties to the sky,
An' sparrers, clust'ren roun' the bough,
Mid chatter to the men at plough ;
The blackbird, hoppèn down along
The hedge, da zing the gâyest zong.

130

'Tis sweet, wi' yerly-wakèn eyes
To zee the zun when vust da rise,
Ar, hālen underwood an' lops
Vrom new-plēsh'd hedges ar vrom copse
To snatch oon's nammet down below
A tree wher primruosen da grow,
But ther's noo time the whol dā long
Lik' evemen wi' the blackbird's zong.

Var when my work is al a-done
Avore the zettèn o' the zun,
Then blushèn Jian da wā'k along
The hedge to mit me in the drong,
An' stây till al is dim an' dark
Bezides the ashen tree's white bark.
An' al bezides the blackbird's shrill
An' runnèn evemen-whissle's still.

How in my buoyhood I did rove
Wi' pryèn eyes along the drove,
Var blackbirds' nestes in the quick-
Set hedges high, an' green, an' thick ;
Ar clim' al up, wi' clingèn knees,
Var crows' nestes in swayen trees,
While frighten'd blackbirds down below
Did chatter o' ther well-know'd foe.

An' we da hear the blackbirds zing
Ther sweetest ditties in the spring,
When nippèn win's na muore da blow
Vrom narthern skies wi' sleet ar snow,

But drēve light doust along between
The cluose leane-hedges, thick an' green ;
An' zoo th' blackbird down along
The hedge da zing the gâyest zong.

William Barnes

Song

PACK, clouds, away, and welcome day,
    With night we banish sorrow ;
Sweet air, blow soft, mount, larks, aloft
    To give my Love good-morrow !
Wings from the wind to please her mind,
    Notes from the lark I'll borrow ;
Bird, prune thy wing, nightingale, sing,
    To give my Love good-morrow ;
        To give my Love good-morrow
        Notes from them both I'll borrow.

Wake from thy nest, Robin red-breast,
    Sing, birds, in every furrow ;
And from each hill, let music shrill
    Give my fair Love good-morrow !
Blackbird and thrush in every bush,
    Stare, linnet, and cock-sparrow !
You pretty elves, amongst yourselves
    Sing my fair Love good-morrow ;
        To give my Love good-morrow
        Sing, birds, in every furrow !

Thomas Heywood.

BENEATH these fruit-tree boughs that shed
   Their snow-white blossoms on my head,
With brightest sunshine round me spread
   Of Spring's unclouded weather,
In this sequester'd nook how sweet
To sit upon my orchard-seat !
And flowers and birds once more to greet,
   My last year's friends together.

One have I mark'd, the happiest guest
In all this covert of the blest :
Hail to Thee, far above the rest
   In joy of voice and pinion !
Thou, Linnet ! in thy green array
Presiding Spirit here to-day
Dost lead the revels of the May,
   And this is thy dominion.

While birds, and butterflies, and flowers,
Make all one band of paramours,
Thou, ranging up and down the bowers
   Art sole in thy employment ;
A Life, a Presence like the air,
Scattering thy gladness without care,
Too blest with any one to pair,
   Thyself thy own enjoyment.

Amid yon tuft of hazel trees
That twinkle to the gusty breeze,

Behold him perch'd in ecstasies
    Yet seeming still to hover;
There, where the flutter of his wings
Upon his back and body flings
Shadows and sunny glimmerings,
    That cover him all over.

My dazzled sight he oft deceives—
A brother of the dancing leaves;
Then flits, and from the cottage-eaves
    Pours forth his song in gushes,
As if by that exulting strain
He mock'd and treated with disdain
The voiceless Form he chose to feign
    While fluttering in the bushes.

W. Wordsworth

Philomela ◌ ◌ ◌ ◌ ◌ ◌

HARK! ah, the Nightingale!
    The tawny-throated!
Hark! from that moonlit cedar what a burst!
What triumph! hark!—what pain!

O Wanderer from a Grecian shore,
Still, after many years, in distant lands,
Still nourishing in thy bewilder'd brain
That wild, unquench'd, deep-sunken, old-world pain—

Say, will it never heal?
And can this fragrant lawn
With its cool trees, and night,
And the sweet, tranquil Thames,
And moonshine, and the dew,
To thy rack'd heart and brain
　　Afford no balm?

　　Dost thou to-night behold
Here, through the moonlight on the English grass,
The unfriendly palace in the Thracian wilds?
　　Dost thou again peruse
With hot cheeks and sear'd eyes
The too clear web, and thy dumb Sister's shame?
　　Dost thou once more assay
Thy flight, and feel come over thee,
Poor Fugitive, the feathery change
Once more, and once more seem to make resound
With love and hate, triumph and agony,
Lone Daulis, and the high Cephissian vale?
　　　Listen, Eugenia—
How thick the bursts come crowding through the
　　　leaves!
　　Again—thou hearest!
Eternal Passion!
Eternal Pain!

Matthew Arnold.

M^Y heart aches, and a drowsy numbness pains
    My sense, as though of hemlock I had drunk,
Or emptied some dull opiate to the drains
    One minute past, and Lethe-wards had sunk :
'Tis not through envy of thy happy lot,
    But being too happy in thine happiness,—
        That thou, light-winged Dryad of the trees,
            In some melodious plot
    Of beechen green, and shadows numberless,
        Singest of summer in full throated ease.

O, for a draught of vintage ! that hath been
    Cool'd a long age in the deep-delved earth,
Tasting of Flora and the country green,
    Dance, and Provençal song, and sunburnt mirth !
O for a beaker full of the warm South,
    Full of the true, the blushful Hippocrene,
        With beaded bubbles winking at the brim,
            And purple-stained mouth ;
    That I might drink, and leave the world unseen,
        And with thee fade away into the forest dim :

Fade far away, dissolve, and quite forget
    What thou among the leaves hast never known,
The weariness, the fever, and the fret
    Here, where men sit and hear each other groan ;
Where palsy shakes a few sad, last gray hairs,
    Where youth grows pale, and spectre-thin, and dies ;

Where but to think is to be full of sorrow
　　　And leaden-eyed despairs,
　Where Beauty cannot keep her lustrous eyes,
　　　Or new Love pine at them beyond to-morrow.

Away! away! for I will fly to thee,
　Not charioted by Bacchus and his pards,
But on the viewless wings of Poesy,
　Though the dull brain perplexes and retards:
Already with thee! tender is the night,
　　And haply the Queen-Moon is on her throne,
　　　Cluster'd around by all her starry Fays;
　　　　But here there is no light,
　　Save what from heaven is with the breezes blown
　　　Through verdurous glooms and winding mossy
　　　　ways.

I cannot see what flowers are at my feet,
　Nor what soft incense hangs upon the boughs,
But, in embalmed darkness, guess each sweet
　Wherewith the seasonable month endows
The grass, the thicket, and the fruit-tree wild;
　White hawthorn, and the pastoral eglantine;
　　Fast-fading violets cover'd up in leaves;
　　　And mid-May's eldest child,
　The coming musk-rose, full of dewy wine,
　　The murmurous haunt of flies on summer eves.

Darkling I listen; and, for many a time
　I have been half in love with easeful Death,
Call'd him soft names in many a mused rhyme,
　To take into the air my quiet breath;

Now more than ever seems it rich to die,
    To cease upon the midnight with no pain,
        While thou art pouring forth thy soul abroad
            In such an ecstasy!
    Still wouldst thou sing, and I have ears in vain—
        To thy high requiem become a sod.

Thou wast not born for death, immortal Bird!
    No hungry generations tread thee down;
The voice I hear this passing night was heard
    In ancient days by emperor and clown:
Perhaps the self-same song that found a path
    Through the sad heart of Ruth, when, sick for home
        She stood in tears amid the alien corn;
            The same that oft-times hath
Charm'd magic casements, opening on the foam
    Of perilous seas, in faery lands forlorn.

Forlorn! the very word is like a bell
    To toll me back from thee to my sole self!
Adieu! the fancy cannot cheat so well
    As she is fam'd to do, deceiving elf.
Adieu! adieu! thy plaintive anthem fades
    Past the near meadows, over the still stream,
        Up the hill-side; and now 'tis buried deep
            In the next valley-glades.
    Was it a vision, or a waking dream.
        Fled is that music :—Do I wake or sleep?

John Keats.

OVER the shoulders and slopes of the dune
    I saw the white daisies go down to the sea,
A host in the sunshine, an army in June,
The people God sends us to set our heart free.

The bobolinks rallied them up from the dell,
The orioles whistled them out of the wood ;
And all of their saying was, " Earth, it is well ! "
And all of their dancing was, " Life, thou art good ! "
Bliss Carman.

To the Daisy ✧ ✧ ✧ ✧ ✧

WITH little here to do or see
    Of things that in the great world be,
Sweet Daisy ! oft I talk to thee,
    For thou art worthy :
Thou unassuming common-place
Of nature with that homely face,
And yet with something of a grace,
    Which love makes for thee !

Oft do I sit by thee at ease,
And weave a web of similes,
Loose types of things through all degrees,
    Thoughts of thy raising :

And many a fond and idle name
I give to thee, for praise or blame,
As is the humour of the game,
    While I am gazing.

A nun demure, of lowly port ;
Or sprightly maiden of love's court,
In thy simplicity the sport
    Of all temptations ;
A queen in crown of rubies dress'd ;
A starveling in a scanty vest ;
Are all, as seem to suit thee best,
    Thy appellations.

A little Cyclops, with one eye
Staring to threaten and defy—
That thought comes next—and instantly
    The freak is over.
The shape will vanish, and behold !
A silver shield with boss of gold,
That spreads itself, some fairy bold
    In fight to cover.

I see thee glittering from afar ;—
And then thou art a pretty star
Not quite so fair as many are
    In heaven above thee !
Yet like a star, with glittering crest,
Self-poised in air, thou seem'st to rest ;
May peace come never to his nest
    Who shall reprove thee !

Sweet flower ! for by that name at last,
When all my reveries are past,
I call thee, and to that cleave fast,
    Sweet silent creature !
That breath'st with me in sun and air,
Do thou, as thou art wont, repair
My heart with gladness, and a share
    Of thy meek nature !

                        William Wordsworth.

To Daffodils ∽ ∽ ∽ ∽

FAIR Daffodils, we weep to see
        You haste away so soon :
As yet the early-rising sun
    Has not attained his noon.
            Stay, stay,
        Until the hasting day
                Has run
        But to the evensong,
And, having prayed together, we
    Will go with you along.

We have short time to stay as you,
    We have as short a spring,
As quick a growth to meet decay,
    As you, or anything.
            We die,

141

As your hours do, and dry
Away,
Like to the summer's rain,
Or as the pearls of morning's dew,
Ne'er to be found again.

Robert Herrick.

I Wandered Lonely as a Cloud

I WANDERED lonely as a cloud
That floats on high o'er vales and hills,
When all at once I saw a crowd,
A host, of golden daffodils;
Beside the lake, beneath the trees,
Fluttering and dancing in the breeze.

Continuous as the stars that shine
And twinkle on the milky way,
They stretched in never-ending line
Along the margin of a bay:
Ten thousand saw I at a glance,
Tossing their heads in sprightly dance.

The waves beside them danced; but they
Out-did the sparkling waves in glee:
A poet could not but be gay,
In such a jocund company:
I gazed—and gazed—but little thought
What wealth the show to me had brought:

For oft, when on my couch I lie
In vacant or in pensive mood,
They flash upon that inward eye
Which is the bliss of solitude ;
And then my heart with pleasure fills,
And dances with the daffodils.

William Wordsworth.

Perdita's Gifts

PERDITA. Here's flowers for you :
   Hot lavender, mints, savory, marjoram ;
The marigold, that goes to bed with the sun,
And with him rises weeping ; these are flowers
Of middle summer, and, I think, they are given
To men of middle age : You are very welcome.
   Camillo. I should leave grazing, were I of your flock,
And only live by gazing.
   Perdita. Out, alas !
You'd be so lean, that blasts of January
Would blow you through and through.—Now, my
   fairest friend,
I would I had some flowers o' the spring, that might
Become your time of day ; and yours ; and yours
That wear upon your virgin branches yet
Your maidenheads growing.—O Proserpina,
For the flowers now, that, frighted, thou let'st fall
From Dis's waggon !—daffodils,
That come before the swallow dares, and take
The winds of March with beauty ; violets, dim,

But sweeter than the lids of Juno's eyes,
Or Cytherea's breath ; pale primroses,
That die unmarried ere they can behold
Bright Phœbus in his strength, a malady
Most incident to maids ; bold oxlips, and
The crown-imperial; lilies of all kinds,
The flower-de-luce being one !   O, these I lack
To make you garlands of ; and, my sweet friend,
To strew him o'er and o'er.

   Florizel. What ! like a corse?

   Perdita. No, like a bank, for love to lie and play
     on :
Not like a corse : or if,—not to be buried,
But quick, and in mine arms.   Come, take your flowers :
Methinks I play as I have seen them do
In Whitsun' pastorals : sure, this robe of mine
Does change my disposition.

   Florizel. What you do
Still betters what is done.   When you speak, sweet,
I'd have you do it ever : when you sing,
I'd have you buy and sell so ; so give alms ;
Pray so ; and, for the ordering your affairs,
To sing them too : when you do dance, I wish you
A wave o' the sea, that you might ever do
Nothing but that ; move still, still so, and own
No other function : each your doing,
So singular in each particular,
Crowns what you are doing in the present deeds,
That all your acts are queens.

William Shakespeare.

WHY do ye weep, sweet babes? can tears
     Speak grief in you,
     Who were but born
  Just as the modest morn
  Teem'd her refreshing dew?
Alas, you have not known that shower
     That mars a flower,
     Nor felt th' unkind
  Breath of a blasting wind,
  Nor are ye worn with years ;
     Or warp'd as we,
  Who think it strange to see
Such pretty flowers, like to orphans young,
To speak by tears, before ye have a tongue.

Speak, whimp'ring younglings, and make known
     The reason why
     Ye droop and weep ;
  Is it for want of sleep,
  Or childish lullaby?
Or that ye have not seen as yet
     The violet?
     Or brought a kiss
  From that Sweet-heart, to this?
  —No, no, this sorrow shown
     By your tears shed,
  Would have this lecture read.

That things of greatest, so of meanest worth,
Conceived with grief are, and with tears brought forth.

Robert Herrick.

Child's Song in Spring

THE silver birch is a dainty lady,
    She wears a satin gown ;
The elm tree makes the old church shady,
    She will not live in town.

The English oak is a sturdy fellow,
    He gets his green coat late ;
The willow is smart in a suit of yellow,
    While brown the beech trees wait.

Such a gay green gown God gives the larches—
    As green as He is good !
The hazels hold up their arms for arches
    When Spring rides through the wood.

The chestnut's proud, and the lilac's pretty,
    The poplar's gentle and tall,
But the plane tree's kind to the poor dull city—
    I love him best of all !

E. Nesbit.

Under the Oak

LOFTY-HUNG boughs of the tall oak, a shadowy height over men that take shelter from the fierce heat, fair-foliaged, closer-roofing than tiles, houses of wood-pigeons, houses of crickets, O noontide branches, protect me likewise who lie beneath your tresses, fleeing from the sun's rays.

Antiphilus.

(J. W. Mackail's translation.)

The Woodlands

O SPREAD agen your leaves an' flow'rs,
　　Luonesome woodlands! zunny woodlands!
Here undernēath the dewy show'rs
　　O warm-âir'd spring-time, zunny woodlands.
As when, in drong ar oben groun',
Wi' happy buoyish heart I voun'
The twitt'ren birds a' builden roun'
　　Your high-bough'd hedges, zunny woodlands.

Ya gie'd me life, ya gie'd me jày,
　　Luonesome woodlands, zunny woodlands ;
Ya gie'd me health as in my plây
　　I rambled droo ye, zunny woodlands.
Ya gie'd me freedom var to rove
In âiry meäd, ar shiady grove ;
Ya gie'd me smilen Fanny's love,
　　The best ov al ō't, zunny woodlands.

147

My vust shrill skylark whiver'd high,
  Luonesome woodlands, zunny woodlands.
To zing below your deep-blue sky
  An' white spring-clouds, O zunny woodlands,
An' boughs o' trees that oonce stood here,
Wer glossy green the happy year
That gie'd me oon I lov'd so dear
  An' now ha lost, O zunny woodlands.

O let me rove agen unspied,
  Luonesome woodlands, zunny woodlands,
Along your green-bough'd hedges' zide,
  As then I rambled, zunny woodlands.
An' wher the missèn trees oonce stood,
Ar tongues oonce rung among the wood,
My memory shall miake em good,
  Though you've a-lost em, zunny woodlands.

William Barnes.

Tapestry Trees ∾　∾　∾　∾　∾

*O*AK. I am the Roof-tree and the Keel .
  I bridge the seas for woe and weal.

Fir. High o'er the lordly oak I stand,
And drive him on from land to land.

Ash I heft my brother's iron bane ;
I shaft the spear and build the wain.

Yew. Dark down the windy dale I grow,
The father of the fateful Bow.

Poplar. The war-shaft and the milking-bowl
I make, and keep the hay-wain whole.

Olive. The King I bless; the lamps I trim;
In my warm wave do fishes swim.

Apple-tree. I bowed my head to Adam's will;
The cups of toiling men I fill.

Vine. I draw the blood from out the earth;
I store the sun for winter mirth.

Orange-tree. Amidst the greenness of my night
My odorous lamps hang round and bright.

Fig-tree. I who am little among trees
In honey-making mate the bees.

Mulberry-tree. Love's lack hath dyed my berries
    red:
For Love's attire my leaves are shed.

Pear-tree. High o'er the mead-flowers' hidden feet
I bear aloft my burden sweet.

Bay. Look on my leafy boughs, the Crown
Of living song and dead renown!

William Morris.

I KNOW that face !
　　In some lone forest place,
When June brings back the laurel to the hills,
　　Where shade and sunlight lace,

　　Where all day long
　　The brown birds make their song—
A music that seems never to have known
　　Dismay nor haste nor wrong—

　　I once before
　　Have seen thee by the shore,
As if about to shed the flowery guise
　　And be thyself once more.

　　Dear, shy, soft face,
　　With just the elfin trace
That lends thy human beauty the last touch
　　Of wild, elusive grace !

　　Can it be true,
　　A god did once pursue
Thy gleaming beauty through the glimmering wood,
　　Drenched in the Dorian dew,

　　Too mad to stay
　　His hot and headstrong way,
Demented by the fragrance of thy flight,
　　Heedless of thy dismay ?

But I to thee
More gently fond would be,
Nor less a lover woo thee with soft words
And woodland melody;

Take pipe and play
Each forest fear away;
Win thee to idle in the leafy shade
All the long summer day;

Tell thee old tales
Of love, that still avails
More than all mighty things in this great world.
Still wonder works nor fails;

Teach thee new lore,
How to love more and more,
And find the magical delirium
In joys unguessed before.

I would try over
And over to discover
Some wild, sweet, foolish, irresistible
New way to be thy lover—

New, wondrous ways
To fill thy golden days,
Thy lovely pagan body with delight,
Thy loving heart with praise.

151

For I would learn,
Deep in the brookside fern,
The magic of the syrinx whispering low
With bubbly fall and turn ;

Mock every note
Of the green woodbird's throat,
Till some wild strain, impassioned yet serene,
Should form and float

Far through the hills,
Where mellow sunlight fills
The world with joy, and from the purple vines
The brew of life distils.

Ah, then indeed
Thy heart should have no need
To tremble at a footfall in the brake,
And bid thy bright limbs speed.

But night would come,
And I should make thy home
In the deep pines, lit by a yellow star
Hung in the dark blue dome—

A fragrant house
Of woven balsam boughs,
Where the great Cyprian mother should receive
Our warm unsullied vows.

Bliss Carman.

SHERWOOD in the twilight, is Robin Hood
    awake?
Grey and ghostly shadows are gliding through the
    brake ;
Shadows of the dappled deer, dreaming of the morn,
Dreaming of a shadowy man that winds a shadowy
    horn.

Robin Hood is here again : all his merry thieves
Hear a ghostly bugle-note shivering through the
    leaves,
Calling as he used to call, faint and far away,
In Sherwood, in Sherwood, about the break of day.

Merry, merry England has kissed the lips of June :
All the wings of fairyland were here beneath the
    moon ;
Like a flight of rose-leaves fluttering in a mist
Of opal and ruby and pearl and amethyst.

Merry, merry England is waking as of old,
With eyes of blither hazel and hair of brighter gold :
For Robin Hood is here again beneath the bursting
    spray
In Sherwood, in Sherwood, about the break of day.

Love is in the greenwood building him a house
Of wild rose and hawthorn and honeysuckle boughs :
Love is in the greenwood : dawn is in the skies ;
And Marian is waiting with a glory in her eyes.

Hark ! The dazzled laverock climbs the golden steep :
Marian is waiting : is Robin Hood asleep?
Round the fairy grass-rings frolic elf and fay,
In Sherwood, in Sherwood, about the break of day.

Oberon, Oberon, rake away the gold,
Rake away the red leaves, roll away the mould,
Rake away the gold leaves, roll away the red,
And wake Will Scarlett from his leafy forest bed.

Friar Tuck and Little John are riding down together
With quarter-staff and drinking-can and grey goose
    feather ;
The dead are coming back again ; the years are rolled
    away
In Sherwood, in Sherwood, about the break of day.

Softly over Sherwood the south wind blows ;
All the heart of England hid in every rose
Hears across the greenwood the sunny whisper leap,
Sherwood in the red dawn, is Robin Hood asleep?

Hark, the voice of England wakes him as of old
And, shattering the silence with a cry of brighter gold,
Bugles in the greenwood echo from the steep,
Sherwood in the red dawn, is Robin Hood asleep?

Where the deer are gliding down the shadowy glen
All across the glades of fern he calls his merry men ;
Doublets of the Lincoln green glancing through the
    May
In Sherwood, in Sherwood, about the break of day ;

Calls them and they answer : from aisles of oak and
    ash
Rings the *Follow! Follow!* and the boughs begin
    to crash ;
The ferns begin to flutter and the flowers begin to fly ;
And through the crimson dawning the robber band
    goes by.

Robin! Robin! Robin!   All his merry thieves
Answer as the bugle-note shivers through the leaves :
Calling as he used to call, faint and far away,
In Sherwood, in Sherwood, about the break of day.

Alfred Noyes.

The Poet in the Woods

EV'N in the spring and playtime of the year,
        That calls the unwonted villager abroad
With all her little ones, a sportive train,
To gather king-cups in the yellow mead,
And prink their hair with daisies, or to pick
A cheap but wholesome salad from the brook,
These shades are all my own.   The tim'rous hare,
Grown so familiar with her frequent guest,
Scarce shuns me ; and the stock-dove unalarmed
Sits cooing in the pine-tree, nor suspends
His long love-ditty for my near approach.
Drawn from his refuge in some lonely elm
That age or injury has hollowed deep,

Where on his bed of wool and matted leaves
He has outslept the winter, ventures forth
To frisk awhile, and bask in the warm sun,
The squirrel, flippant, pert, and full of play.
He sees me, and at once, swift as a bird,
Ascends the neighb'ring beech ; there whisks his
    brush,
And perks his ears, and stamps and scolds aloud,
With all the prettiness of feigned alarm,
And anger insignificantly fierce.

William Cowper.

On Solitude

HAIL, old patrician trees, so great and good !
    Hail, ye plebeian underwood !
    Where the poetic birds rejoice,
And for their quiet nests and plenteous food,
    Pay with their grateful voice.

Hail, the poor muse's richest manor seat !
    Ye country houses and retreat,
    Which all the happy gods so love,
That for you oft they quit their bright and great
    Metropolis above.

Here nature does a house for me erect,
    Nature the wisest architect,
    Who those fond artists does despise
That can the fair and living trees neglect,
    Yet the dead timber prize.

Here let me careless and unthoughtful lying,
Hear the soft winds above me flying
With all their wanton boughs dispute,
And the more tuneful birds to both replying,
Nor be myself too mute.

A silver stream shall roll his waters near,
Gilt with the sunbeams here and there,
On whose enamel'd bank I'll walk,
And see how prettily they smile, and hear
How prettily they talk.

Ah wretched, and too solitary he
Who loves not his own company!
He'll feel the weight of 't many a day
Unless he call in sin or vanity
To help to bear 't away.

O Solitude, first state of human-kind!
Which blest remain'd till man did find
Even his own helper's company.
As soon as two (alas!) together join'd,
The serpent made up three.

The god himself, through countless ages thee
His sole companion chose to be,
Thee, sacred Solitude alone,
Before the branchy head of number's tree
Sprang from the trunk of one.

157

Thou (though men think thine an unactive part)
    Dost break and tame th' unruly heart,
    Which else would know no settled pace,
Making it more well manag'd by thy art
    With swiftness and with grace.

Thou the faint beams of reason's scatter'd light,
    Dost like a burning-glass unite,
    Dost multiply the feeble heat,
And fortify the strength, till thou dost bright
    And noble fires beget.

Whilst this hard truth I teach, methinks, I see
    The monster London laugh at me,
    I should at thee too, foolish city,
If it were fit to laugh at misery,
    But thy estate I pity.

Let but thy wicked men from out thee go,
    And all the fools that crowd thee so,
    Even thou who dost thy millions boast,
A village less than Islington wilt grow,
    A solitude almost.

                Abraham Cowley.

An Invocation

I NEVER prayed for Dryads, to haunt the woods
  again ;
More welcome were the presence of hungering, thirsting men,
Whose doubts we could unravel, whose hopes we could
  fulfil,
Our wisdom tracing backward, the river to the rill ;
Were such beloved forerunners one summer day
  restored,
Then, then we might discover the Muse's mystic
  hoard.

Oh, dear divine Comatas, I would that thou and I
Beneath this broken sunlight this leisure day might
  lie ;
Where trees from distant forests, whose names were
  strange to thee,
Should bend their amorous branches within thy
  reach to be,
And flowers thine Hellas knew not, which art hath
  made more fair,
Should shed their shining petals upon thy fragrant
  hair.

Then thou shouldst calmly listen with ever-changing
  looks
To songs of younger minstrels and plots of modern
  books

And wonder at the daring of poets later born,

Whose thoughts are unto thy thoughts as noon-tide is
to morn ;

And little shouldst thou grudge them their greater
strength of soul,

Thy partners in the torch-race, though nearer to the
goal.

As when ancestral portraits look gravely from the
walls

Upon the youthful baron who treads their echoing
halls ;

And whilst he builds new turrets, the thrice ennobled
heir

Would gladly wake his grandsire his home and feast
to share ;

So from Ægean laurels that hide their ancient urn

I fain would call thee hither, my sweeter lore to learn.

Or in thy cedarn prison thou waitest for the bee :

Ah, leave that simple honey, and take thy food from
me.

My sun is stooping westward. Entrancèd dreamer,
haste :

There's fruitage in my garden, that I would have
thee taste.

Now lift the lid a moment : now, Dorian shepherd,
speak :

Two minds shall flow together, the English and the
Greek.

William Cory.

Song   ᴑ   ᴑ   ᴑ   ᴑ   ᴑ   ᴑ

U NDER the greenwood tree,
    Who loves to lie with me,
And tune his merry throat
Unto the sweet bird's note,
Come hither, come hither, come hither !
    Here shall he see
    No enemy
But winter and rough weather.

    Who doth ambition shun,
    And loves to live i' the sun,
Seeking the food he eats,
And pleased with what he gets,
Come hither, come hither, come hither !
    Here shall he see
    No enemy
But winter and rough weather.

                 William Shakespeare.

O Dreamy, Gloomy, Friendly Trees   ᴑ   ᴑ

O DREAMY, gloomy, friendly trees
    I came along your narrow track
To bring my gifts unto your knees,
    And gifts did you give back.
For when I brought this heart that burns,
    These thoughts that bitterly repine,
And laid them here amidst the ferns
    And the hum of boughs divine,

Ye, vastest breathers of the air,
  Shook down with slow and mighty poise
Your coolness on the human care,
  Your wonder on its toys,
Your greenness on the heart's despair,
  Your darkness on its noise.

Herbert Trench.

A Ballad of Trees and the Master

INTO the woods my Master went,
  Clean forspent, forspent.
Into the woods my Master came,
Forspent with love and shame.
But the olives were not blind to Him,
The little gray leaves were kind to Him:
The thorn-tree had a mind to Him
When into the woods He came.

Out of the woods my Master went,
And He was well content.
Out of the woods my Master came,
Content with death and shame.
When Death and Shame would woo Him last,
From under the trees they drew Him last:
'Twas on a tree they slew Him—last
When out of the woods He came.

Sidney Lanier.

SUMMER SPORTS AND PASTIMES

A BOY'S PRAYER

God who created me
　Nimble and light of limb,
In three elements free,
　To run, to ride, to swim :
　Not when the sense is dim,
But now from the heart of joy,
　I would remember Him :
Take the thanks of a boy.

H. C. Beeching.

The Angler's Rest

*C*ORIDON. I will sing a song, if anybody will sing another; else, to be plain with you, I will sing none: I am none of those that sing for meat, but for company: I say, "'Tis merry in hall when men sing all."

Piscator. I'll promise you I'll sing a song that was lately made at my request by Mr. William Basse— one that hath made the choice songs of the "Hunter in his career," and of "Tom of Bedlam," and many others of note; and this that I will sing is in praise of angling.

Coridon. And then mine shall be the praise of a countryman's life: what will the rest sing of?

Peter. I will promise you I will sing another song in praise of angling to-morrow night; for we will not part till then, but fish to-morrow, and sup together, and the next day every man leave fishing, and fall to his business.

Venator. 'Tis a match; and I will provide you a song or a catch against then, too, which shall give some addition of mirth to the company; for we will be civil and as merry as beggars.

Piscator. 'Tis a match, my masters: let's e'en say grace, and turn to the fire, drink the other cup to wet our whistles, and so sing away all sad thoughts.

Come on, my masters, who begins? I think it is best to draw cuts, and avoid contention.

Peter. It is a match. Look, the shortest cut falls to Coridon.

Coridon. Well, then, I will begin, for I hate contention.

CORIDON'S SONG

Oh, the sweet contentment
The countryman doth find!
    Heigh trolollie lollie loe,
    Heigh trolollie lollie iee.
That quiet contemplation
Possesseth all my mind;
    Then care away,
    And wend along with me.

For Courts are full of flattery,
As hath too oft been tried;
    Heigh trolollie lollie loe, etc.
The city full of wantonness,
And both are full of pride:
    Then care away, etc.

But, oh! the honest countryman
Speaks truly from his heart;
   Heigh trolollie lollie loe, etc.
His pride is in his tillage,
His horses and his cart;
   Then care away, etc.

Our clothing is good sheep-skins,
Grey russet for our wives;
   Heigh trolollie lollie loe, etc.
'Tis warmth, and not gay clothing,
That doth prolong our lives;
   Then care away, etc.

The ploughman, though he labour hard,
Yet on the holiday,
   Heigh trolollie lollie loe, etc.
No emperor so merrily
Doth pass his time away;
   Then care away, etc.

To recompense our tillage,
The heavens afford us showers;
   Heigh trolollie lollie loe, etc.
And for our sweet refreshments
The earth affords us bowers:
   Then care away, etc.

The cuckoo and the nightingale
Full merrily do sing,

Heigh trolollie lollie loe, etc.
And with their pleasant roundelays
Bid welcome to the spring ;
    Then care away, etc.

This is not half the happiness
The countryman enjoys ;
    Heigh trolollie lollie loe, etc.
Though others think they have as much,
Yet he that says so lies ;
    Then come away, turn
    Countryman with me.—*Jo. Chalkhill.*

Piscator. Well sung, Coridon ! this song was sung
with mettle, and it was choicely fitted to the occasion ;
I shall love you for it as long as I know you.   I would
you were a brother of the angle : for a companion
that is cheerful, and free from swearing and scurrilous
discourse, is worth gold.   I love such mirth as does
not make friends ashamed to look upon one another
next morning ; nor men that cannot well bear it, to
repent the money they spend when they be warmed
with drink : and take this for a rule, you may pick out
such times and such companions, that you may make
yourselves merrier for a little than a great deal of
money ; for "'Tis the company and not the charge
that makes the feast" : and such a companion you
prove, I thank you for it.

But I will not compliment you out of the debt that

I owe you; and therefore I will begin my song, and wish it may be so well liked.

THE ANGLER'S SONG

As inward love breeds outward talk,
The hound some praise, and some the hawk;
Some, better pleased with private sport,
Use tennis; some a mistress court:
    But these delights I neither wish
    Nor envy, while I freely fish.

Who hunts, doth oft in danger ride;
Who hawks, lures oft both far and wide;
Who uses games shall often prove
A loser; but who falls in love
    Is fetter'd in fond Cupid's snare:
    My angle breeds me no such care.

Of recreation there is none
So free as fishing is alone;
All other pastimes do no less
Than mind and body both possess;
    My hand alone my work can do
    So I can fish and study too.

I care not, I, to fish in seas—
Fresh rivers best my mind do please,
Whose sweet calm course I contemplate,
And seek in life to imitate:
    In civil bounds I fain would keep.
    And for my past offences weep.

And when the timorous trout I wait
To take, and he devours my bait,
How poor a thing, sometimes I find,
Will captivate a greedy mind ;
    And when none bite, I praise the wise,
    Whom vain allurements ne'er surprise.

But yet, though while I fish I fast,
I make good fortune my repast ;
And thereunto my friend invite,
In whom I more than that delight ;
    Who is more welcome to my dish
    Than to my angle was my fish.

As well content no prize to take,
As use of taken prize to make :
For so our Lord was pleasèd, when
He fishers made fishèrs of men :
    Where (which is in no other game)
    A man may fish and praise His name.

The first men that our Saviour dear
Did choose to wait upon Him here,
Bless'd fishers were, and fish the last
Food was that He on earth did taste :
    I therefore strive to follow those
    Whom He to follow Him hath chose.

Coridon. Well sung, brother ! you have paid your
debt in good coin. We anglers are all beholden to

the good man that made this song : come, hostess, give us more ale and let's drink to him.

Izaak Walton.

The Angler's Virtues

NOW for the inward qualities of the minde ; albeit some writers reduce them to twelve heads, which indeed whosoever enjoyeth, cannot chuse but be very compleat in much perfection, yet I must draw them into many more branches. The first, and most especial whereof is, that a skilful angler ought to be a general scoller, and seen in all the Liberal Sciences, as a Grammarian to know how either to write or discourse of his art in true and fitting terms, either without affectation or rudeness. He should have sweetness of speech, to perswade and entice others to delight in an exercise so much laudable. He should have strength of arguments to defend and maintain his profession, against envy or slander.

He should have knowledge in the Sun, Moon, and Stars, that by their aspects he may guesse the seasonableness or unseasonableness of the weather, the breeding of storms, and from what coasts the winds are ever delivered. He should be a good knower of countries, and well used to High-wayes, that by taking the readiest paths to every Lake, Brook and River, his Journies may be more certain and less wearisome. He should have knowledge in propor-

tions of all sorts, whether Circular, Square, or Dia-
metrical, that when he shall be questioned of his
diurnal progresses, he may give a Geographical
description of the angles and channels of Rivers,
how they fall from their heads, and what compasses
they fetch in their several windings. He must also
have the perfect art of numbring, that in the sounding of Lakes or Rivers, he may know how many foot
or inches each severally containeth ; and by adding,
subtracting or multiplying the same, he may yield
the reason of every River's swift or slow current. He
should not be unskilful in Musick, that whensoever
either melancholy, heaviness of his thoughts, or the
perturbations of his own fancies, stirreth up sadness
in him, he may remove the same with some godly
Hymn or Anthem, of which *David* gives him ample
examples.

Gervase Markham.

The Angler's Poesy

AND I do easily believe, that peace and patience,
and a calm content, did cohabit in the cheerful
heart of Sir Henry Wotton ; because I know that
when he was beyond seventy years of age he made
this description of a part of the present pleasure that
possessed him, as he sat quietly in a summer's
evening, on a bank, a-fishing. It is a description of

the spring ; which, because it glided as soft and sweetly from his pen, as that river does at this time, by which it was then made, I shall repeat it unto you :

This day dame Nature seem'd in love ;
The lusty sap began to move ;
Fresh juice did stir th' embracing vines ;
And birds had drawn their valentines.
The jealous trout, that low did lie,
Rose at a well-dissembled fly ;
There stood my friend, with patient skill,
Attending of his trembling quill ;
Already were the eaves possess'd
With the swift Pilgrim's daubèd nest ;
The groves already did rejoice
In Philomel's triumphing voice,
The showers were short, the weather mild,
The morning fresh, the evening smiled.
  Joan takes her neat-rubbed pail, and now
She trips to milk the sand-red cow ;
Where, for some sturdy foot-ball swain,
Joan strokes a syllabub or twain.
The fields and gardens were beset
With tulips, crocus, violet ;
And now, though late, the modest rose
Did more than half a blush disclose.
    Thus all looks gay and full of cheer,
    To welcome the new-livery'd year.

These were the thoughts that then possessed the undisturbed mind of Sir Henry Wotton. Will you hear the wish of another angler, and the commendation of his happy life, which he also sings in verse? viz., Jo. Davors, Esq. :

Let me live harmlessly ; and near the brink
   Of Trent or Avon have a dwelling-place,
Where I may see my quill or cork down sink
   With eager bite of perch, or bleak, or dace ;
And on the world and my Creator think :
   Whilst some men strive ill-gotten goods t' embrace
And others spend their time in base excess
Of wine, or worse, in war and wantonness.

Let them that list, these pastimes still pursue,
   And on such pleasing fancies feed their fill :
So I the fields and meadows green may view,
   And daily by fresh rivers walk at will,
Among the daisies and the violets blue,
   Red hyacinth and yellow daffodil,
Purple narcissus like the morning rays,
Pale gander-grass, and azure culverkeys.

I count it higher pleasure to behold
   The stately compass of the lofty sky ;
And in the midst thereof, like burning gold,
   The flaming chariot of the world's great eye ;
The watery clouds that, in the air up-roll'd,
   With sundry kinds of painted colours fly ;
And fair Aurora, lifting up her head,
Still blushing, rise from old Tithonus' bed :

The hills and mountains raisèd from the plains,
    The plains extended level with the ground ;
The grounds divided into sundry veins,
    The veins enclos'd with rivers running round ;
These rivers making way through nature's chains
    With headlong course into the sea profound ;
The raging sea, beneath the valleys low,
Where lakes and rills and rivulets do flow ;

The lofty woods, the forests wide and long,
    Adorn'd with leaves and branches fresh and green,
In whose cool bowers the birds, with many a song,
    Do welcome with their choir the summer's queen ;
The meadows fair, where Flora's gifts among
    Are intermix'd with verdant grass between ;
The silver-scalèd fish that softly swim
Within the sweet brook's crystal watery stream.

All these, and many more of His creation
    That made the heavens, the angler oft doth see ;
Taking therein no little delectation,
    To think how strange, how wonderful they be !
Framing thereof an inward contemplation
    To set his heart from other fancies free ;
And whilst he looks on these with joyful eye,
His mind is wrapt above the starry sky.

Sir, I am glad my memory has not lost these last
verses, because they are somewhat more pleasant and
more suitable to May-day than my harsh discourse.

                                        Izaak Walton.

The South Wind ∽ ∽ ∽ ∽

A Fisherman's Blessings

O BLESSED drums of Aldershot !
O blessed South-west train !
O blessed, blessed Speaker's clock,
All prophesying rain !

O blessed yaffil, laughing loud !
O blessed falling glass !
O blessed fan of cold gray cloud !
O blessed smelling grass !

O bless'd South wind that toots his horn
Through every hole and crack !
I'm off at eight to-morrow morn
To bring *such* fishes back !

Charles Kingsley.

Old Match Days ∽ ∽ ∽ ∽ ∽

THERE was high feasting held on Broad-Half-
penny during the solemnity of one of our grand
matches. Oh ! it was a heart-stirring sight to witness
the multitude forming a complete and dense circle
round that noble green. Half the county would be
present, and all their hearts with us.—Little Hambledon, pitted against all England, was a proud thought

for the Hampshire men. Defeat was glory in such a struggle—Victory, indeed, made us only "a little lower than angels." How those fine brawn-faced fellows of farmers would drink to our success! And then what stuff they had to drink!—Punch!—not your new *Ponche à la Romaine*, or *Ponche à la Groseille*, or your modern cat-lap milk punch—punch be-deviled; but good, unsophisticated, John Bull stuff —stark!—that would stand on end—punch that would make a cat speak! Sixpence a bottle! We had not sixty millions of interest to pay in those days. The ale, too!—not the modern horror under the same name, that drives as many men melancholy-mad as the hypocrites do;—not the beastliness of these days, that will make a fellow's inside like a shaking bog, and as rotten; but barley-corn, such as would put the souls of three butchers into one weaver. Ale that would flare like turpentine—genuine Boniface!—This immortal viand (for it was more than liquor) was vended at twopence per pint. The immeasurable villany of our vintners would, with their march of intellect (if ever they could get such a brewing), drive a pint of it out into a gallon. Then the quantity the fellows would eat! Two or three of them would strike dismay into a round of beef. They could no more have pecked in that style than they could have flown, had the infernal black stream (that type of Acheron!) which soddens the carcass of a Londoner, been the fertilizer of their clay. There would this company, consisting most likely of some thousands,

M   177

remain patiently and anxiously watching every turn of fate in the game, as if the event had been the meeting of two armies to decide their liberty. And whenever a Hambledon man made a good hit, worth four or five runs, you would hear the deep mouths of the whole multitude baying away in pure Hampshire —"Go hard!—go hard!—*Tich* and turn!—*tich* and turn!" To the honour of my countrymen, let me bear testimony upon this occasion also, as I have already done upon others. Although their provinciality in general, and personal partialities individually, were naturally interested in behalf of the Hambledon men, I cannot call to recollection an instance of their wilfully stopping a ball that had been hit out among them by one of our opponents. Like *true* Englishmen, they would give an enemy fair play. How strongly are all those scenes, of fifty years by-gone, painted in my memory!—and the smell of that ale comes upon me as freshly as the new May flowers.

John Nyren.

The Cricket Ball Sings   ᘒ   ᘒ   ᘒ   ᘒ

LEATHER—the heart o' me, leather—the rind
   o' me,
  O but the soul of me's other than that!
Else, should I thrill as I do so exultingly
  Climbing the air from the thick of the bat?

Leather—the heart o' me : ay, but in verity
  Kindred I claim with the sun in the sky.
Heroes, bow all to the little red ball,
  And bow to my brother ball blazing on high.

> Pour on us torrents of light, good Sun,
>   Shine in the hearts of my cricketers, shine ;
> Fill them with gladness and might, good Sun,
>   Touch them with glory, O Brother of mine,
>   Brother of mine,
>   Brother of mine !
> We are the lords of them, Brother and Mate,
>   I but a little ball, thou but a Great !

Give me the bowler whose fingers embracing me
  Tingle and throb with the joy of the game,
One who can laugh at a smack to the boundary,
  Single of purpose and steady of aim.
That is the man for me : striving in sympathy,
  Ours is a fellowship sure to prevail.
Willow must fall in the end to the ball—
  See, like a tiger I leap for the bail.

Give me the fieldsman whose eyes never stray from me,
  Eager to clutch me, a roebuck in pace :
Perish the unalert, perish the "buttery,"
  Perish the laggard I strip in the race.
Grand is the ecstasy soaring triumphantly,
  Holding the gaze of the meadow is grand,
Grandest of all to the soul of the ball
  Is the finishing grip of the honest brown hand.

Give me the batsman who squanders his force on me,
  Crowding the strength of his soul in a stroke;
Perish the muff and the little tin Shrewsbury,
  Meanly contented to potter and poke.
He who would pleasure me, he must do doughtily,—
  Bruises and buffetings stir me like wine.
Giants, come all, do your worst with the ball,
  Sooner or later you're mine, sirs, you're mine.

        Pour on us torrents of light, good Sun,
          Shine in the hearts of my cricketers, shine,
        Fill them with gladness and might, good Sun,
          Touch them with glory, O Brother of mine,
            Brother of mine,
            Brother of mine !
        We are the lords of them, Brother and Mate :
        I but a little ball, thou but a Great.

E. V. Lucas.

William Beldham's Memories

"WE used to go as eagerly to a match as if it
   were two armies fighting : we stood at nothing
if masters allowed the time. From our parish to
Hambledon is twenty-seven miles, and we used to
ride both ways the same day, early and late. At last,
I and John Wells were about building a cart : you
have heard of tax carts, sir ; well, the tax was put
on then, and that stopped us. The members of the
Hambledon Club had a caravan to take their Eleven

about : they used once to play always in velvet caps. They are so drawn in an old painting. Lord Winchelsea's Eleven used to play in silver - laced hats ; and the fashionable dress was knee-breeches and stockings. We never thought of knocks ; and, remember, I played against Browne of Brighton too. Certainly, you would see a bump heave under the stocking, and even the blood come through ; but I never knew a man killed, now you ask the question, and I never saw any accident of much consequence, in my long experience, though many an *all but*. . . .

"I remember one match when Ring was playing against David Harris, and the game was much against him, Sir Horace Mann was cutting about with his stick among the daisies, and cheering every run — you would have thought his whole fortune (and he would often bet some hundreds) was staked upon the game—and, as a new man was going in, he went across to Ring, and said, 'Ring, carry your bat through and make up all the runs, and I'll give you £10 a year for life.' Well, Ring was out for sixty runs, and only three to tie, and four to beat, and the last man made them. It was Sir Horace who took Aylward away with him out of Hampshire ; but the best bat made but a poor bailiff, we heard.

"It was said that David Harris once bowled Tom 170 balls for one run ! David was a potter by trade, and in a kind of skittle-alley formed between hurdles, he used to practise by bowling four different balls from one end, and then picking them up he would bowl them back again. His bowling cost him a great deal of practice; but it proved well worth his while, for no man ever bowled like David, and he was always first chosen of all the men in England." *Nil sine labore*, remember, young cricketers all.

"In our days there were no padded gloves. I have seen Tom Walker rub his bleeding fingers in the dust! David used to say he liked to *rind* him. . . .

"I believe that Walker, Fennex, and myself first opened the Old Players' eyes to what could be done with the bat; Walker by cutting, and Fennex and I by forward play: but all improvement was owing to David Harris's bowling. His bowling rose almost perpendicular: it was once pronounced a jerk; it was altogether most extraordinary.—For thirteen years I averaged forty-three a match, though frequently I had only one innings; but I never could half play unless runs were really wanted."

Rev. James Pycroft.

Going Down Hill on a Bicycle

A Boy's Song

W ITH lifted feet, hands still,
    I am poised, and down the hill
Dart, with heedful mind;
    The air goes by in a wind.

Swifter and yet more swift,
Till the heart, with a mighty lift,
Makes the lungs laugh, the throat cry
"O bird, see ; see, bird, I fly.

" Is this, is this your joy,
O bird, then I, though a boy,
For a golden moment share
Your feathery life in air !"

Say, heart, is there aught like this
In a world that is full of bliss?
'Tis more than skating, bound
Steel-shod to the level ground.

Speed slackens now, I float
Awhile in my airy boat :
Till when the wheels scarce crawl,
My feet to the pedals fall.

Alas, that the longest hill
Must end in a vale ; but still,
Who climbs with toil, whereso'er,
Shall find wings waiting there.

H. C. Beeching.

HOW many a time have I
  Cloven with arms still lustier, breast more
    daring,
The wave all roughened ; with a swimmer's stroke
Flinging the billows back from my drench'd hair,
And laughing from my lip the audacious brine,
Which kiss'd it like a wine-cup, rising o'er
The waves as they arose, and prouder still
The loftier they uplifted me ; and oft,
In wantonness of spirit, plunging down
Into their green and glassy gulfs, and making
My way to shells and seaweed, all unseen
By those above, till they waxed fearful ; then
Returning with my grasp full of such tokens
As showed that I had searched the deep : Exulting,
With a far-dashing stroke, and drawing deep
The long-suspended breath, again I spurned
The foam which broke around me, and pursued
My track like a sea-bird.

Lord Byron.

REFRESHMENT AND THE INN

But hark! a sound is stealing on my ear—
    A soft and silvery sound—I know it well.
Its tinkling tells me that a time is near
    Precious to me—it is the Dinner Bell.
O blessed Bell! thou bringest beef and beer,
    Thou bringest good things more than tongue may tell!
Seared is, of course, my heart—but unsubdued
Is, and shall be, my appetite for food.

C. S. Calverley.

And malt does more than Milton can
To justify God's ways to man.

A. E. Housman.

Sweet when the morn is grey,
Sweet when they've cleared away
Lunch, and at close of day
        Possibly sweetest.

C. S. Calverley.

The Respect due to Hunger ᕙ ᕙ ᕙ

I GRANT there is one subject on which it is
pleasant to talk on a journey ; and that is, what
one shall have for supper when we get to our inn at
night. The open air improves this sort of conversa-
tion or friendly altercation, by setting a keener edge
on appetite. Every mile of the road heightens the
flavour of the viands we expect at the end of it. How
fine it is to enter some old town, walled and turreted,
just at the approach of nightfall, or to come to some
straggling village, with the lights streaming through
the surrounding gloom ; and then after inquiring for
the best entertainment that the place affords, to " take
one's ease at one's inn ! " These eventful moments
in our lives' history are too precious, too full of solid,
heartfelt happiness to be frittered and dribbled away
in imperfect sympathy. I would have them all to
myself, and drain them to the last drop : they will do
to talk of or to write about afterwards. What a delicate
speculation it is, after drinking whole goblets of tea,

" The cups that cheer, but not inebriate,"

and letting the fumes ascend into the brain, to sit
considering what we shall have for supper—eggs and
a rasher, a rabbit smothered in onions, or an excellent
veal cutlet! Sancho in such a situation once fixed
upon cow-heel; and his choice, though he could not
help it, is not to be disparaged. Then, in the intervals
of pictured scenery and Shandean contemplation, to
catch the preparation and the stir in the kitchen
—*Procul, O procul, este profani!* These hours
are sacred to silence and to musing, to be trea-
sured up in the memory, and to feed the source
of smiling thoughts hereafter. I would not waste
them in idle talk.

William Hazlitt.

In Praise of Ale

WHEN as the Chilly Rocko blowes
    And Winter tells a heavy tale,
When Pyes and Dawes and Rookes and Crows
Sit cursing of the frosts and snowes;
    Then give me Ale.

Ale in a Saxon Rumken then,
    Such as will make Grim Malkin prate;
Rouseth up valour in all men,
Quickens the Poet's wit and pen,
    Despiseth fate.

Ale that the absent battle fights,
  And frames the march of Swedish drum,
Disputes the Prince's lawes and rights,
And what is past and what's to come
    Tells mortal wights.

Ale that the Plowman's heart up keeps
  And equals it with Tyrants' thrones,
That wipes the eye that over weeps,
And lulls in dainty and sure sleeps
    His wearied bones.

Grandchild of Ceres, Barley's daughter,
  Wine's emulous neighbour though but stale,
Innobling all the Nymphs of water
And filling each man's heart with laughter—
    Ha! Ha! give me Ale!

Old Song.

A Panegyric upon Excellent Strong Beer, which
  he drank at the Town of Wich, in Worcester
  shire, where Salt is made

THOU ever youthful god of wine,
    Whose burnish'd cheeks with rubies shine
Thy brows with ivy chaplets crown'd;
We dare thee here to pledge around.
  Thy wanton grapes we do detest;
  Here's richer juice from barley press'd.

189

Let not the Muses vainly tell,
What virtue's in the horse-hoof well,
That scarce one drop of good blood breeds,
But with mere inspiration feeds :
  Oh let them come and taste this beer,
  And water henceforth they'll forswear.

If that the Paracelsian crew
The virtues of this liquor knew,
Their endless toils they would give o'er,
And never use extractions more.
  'Tis medicine ; meat for young and old :
  Elixir ; blood of tortur'd gold.

It is sublim'd ; it's calcinate ;
'Tis rectified ; precipitate ;
It is Androgena, Sol's wife ;
It is the Mercury of life ;
  It is the quintessence of malt ;
  And they that drink it want no salt.

It heals, it hurts ; it cures, it kills ;
Men's heads with proclamations fills ;
It makes some dumb, and others speak ;
Strong vessels hold, and crack'd ones leak ;
  It makes some rich, and others poor ;
  It makes, and yet mars many a score.
Thomas Nabbes.

THE parapet balustrade round the roof of Castle Ashby, in Northamptonshire, is carved into the letters, "Nisi Dominus custodiat domum, frustra vigilat qui custodit eam." This is not amiss to decipher as you come up the long avenue some summer or autumn day, and to moralise upon afterwards at the little "Rose and Crown" at Yardley, if such good Homebrewed be there as used to be before I knew I was to die.

Edward FitzGerald.

Marie ❧   ❧   ❧   ❧   ❧   ❧

THE Lion d'Or at Quimperlé
   Housed abbots in a holier day;
     And yet the vesper bell
     Means much in an hostel.

Its pensive note moves saint and sinner,
It calls my heart and me to dinner,
     Whereof the plates are plied
     By grace personified.

But she who wields the coffee-pot
(Smiling on some, on others not),
     Ah ! she is more divine
     Than abbey, church, or shrine.

191

Eyes like a moonbeam, and a face
Where dimples run a joyous race—
My friend, if you could see
How she hath smiled on me !

Ah, that I could for ever stay
In the Lion d'Or at Quimperlé !

Henry Bernard.

At the Lepre ✦ ✦ ✦ ✦ ✦

" I WISH you could come to our mess at the 'Lepre.'
It's such a dinner ! such a table-cloth ! such a
waiter ! such a company ! Every man has a beard
and a sombrero : and you would fancy we were a
band of brigands. We are regaled with wood-cocks,
snipes, wild swans, ducks, robins, and owls and
οἰωνοῖσί τε πᾶσι for dinner ; and with three pauls'
worth of wines and victuals the hungriest has enough,
even Claypole the sculptor. Did you ever know him ?
He used to come to the 'Haunt.' He looks like the
Saracen's head with his beard now. There is a
French table still more hairy than ours, a German
table, an American table. After dinner we go and
have coffee and mezzo-caldo at the 'Caffè Greco' over
the way. Mezzo-caldo is not a bad drink ; a little
rum, a slice of fresh citron, lots of pounded sugar,
and boiling water for the rest. Here in various parts
of the cavern (it is a vaulted low place), the various

nations have their assigned quarters, and we drink our coffee and strong waters, and abuse Guido, or Rubens, or Bernini, *selon les goûts*, and blow such a cloud of smoke as would make Warrington's lungs dilate with pleasure. We get very good cigars for a bajocco and a half—that is, very good for us, cheap tobacconalians ; and capital when you have got no others. M'Collop is here : he made a great figure at a cardinal's reception in the tartan of the M'Collop. He is splendid at the tomb of the Stuarts, and wanted to cleave Haggard down to the chine with his claymore for saying that Charles Edward was often drunk."

W. M. Thackeray.

Madeira ～ ～ ～ ～ ～ ～

I FOUND his worship a jolly, red-faced gentleman, of about fifty-five ; he was dressed in a green coat, white corduroy breeches, and drab gaiters, and sat on an old-fashioned leather sofa, with two small thorough-bred English terriers, one on each side of him. He had all the appearance of a genuine old English gentleman who kept good wine in his cellar.

"Sir," said I, "I have brought you a thousand pounds ;" and I said this after the servant had retired, and the two terriers had ceased their barking, which is natural to all such dogs at the sight of a stranger.

And when the magistrate had received the money, and signed and returned a certain paper which I handed to him, he rubbed his hands, and looking very benignantly at me, exclaimed—

"And now, young gentleman, that our business is over, perhaps you can tell me where the fight is to take place?"

"I am sorry, sir," said I, "that I can't inform you, but everybody seems to be anxious about it;" and then I told him what had occurred to me on the road with the ale-house keeper.

"I know him," said his worship; "he's a tenant of mine, and a good fellow, somewhat too much in my debt, though. But how is this, young gentleman, you look as if you had been walking? You did not come on foot?"

"Yes, sir, I came on foot."

"On foot! Why, it is sixteen miles."

"I shan't be tired when I have walked back."

"You can't ride, I suppose?"

"Better than I can walk."

"Then why do you walk?"

"I have frequently to make journeys connected with my profession; sometimes I walk, sometimes I ride, just as the whim takes me."

"Will you take a glass of wine?"

"Yes."

"That's right; what shall it be?"

"Madeira."

The magistrate gave a violent slap on his knee. "I like your taste," said he; "I am fond of a glass of Madeira myself, and can give you such a one as you will not drink every day. Sit down, young gentleman; you shall have a glass of Madeira, and the best I have."

Thereupon he got up, and, followed by his two terriers, walked slowly out of the room.

I looked round the room, and, seeing nothing which promised me much amusement, I sat down, and fell again into my former train of thought.

"What is truth?" said I.

"Here it is," said the magistrate, returning at the end of a quarter of an hour, followed by the servant with a tray; "here's the true thing, or I am no judge, far less a justice. It has been thirty years in my cellar last Christmas. There," said he to the servant, "put it down, and leave my young friend and me to ourselves. Now what do you think of it?"

"It is very good," said I.

"Did you ever taste better Madeira?"

"I never before tasted Madeira."

"Then you ask for a wine without knowing what it is?"

"I ask for it, sir, that I may know what it is."

"Well, there is logic in that, as Parr would say; you have heard of Parr!"

"Old Parr?"

"Yes, old Parr, but not that Parr; you mean the English, I the Greek Parr, as people call him."

"I don't know him."

"Perhaps not—rather too young for that; but were you of my age you might have cause to know him, coming from where you do. He kept school there, I was his first scholar; he flogged Greek into me till I loved him—and he loved me: he came to see me last year, and sat in that chair. I honour Parr—he knows much, and is a sound man."

"Does he know the truth?"

"Know the truth! He knows what's good, from an oyster to an ostrich—he's not only sound but round."

"Suppose we drink his health?"

"Thank you, boy: here's Parr's health, and Whiter's."

"Who is Whiter?"

"Don't you know Whiter? I thought everybody knew Reverend Whiter the philologist, though I suppose you scarcely know what that means. A man fond of tongues and languages, quite out of your way—he understands some twenty; what do you say to that?"

"Is he a sound man?"

"Why, as to that, I scarcely know what to say: he has got queer notions in his head—wrote a book to prove that all words came originally from the earth; who knows? Words have roots, and roots live in the earth; but, upon the whole, I should not call him altogether a sound man, though he can talk nearly as fast as Parr."

"Is he a round man?"

"Ay, boy, rounder than Parr. I'll sing you a song, if you like, which will let you into his character:

> "Give me the haunch of a buck to eat, and to drink Madeira old,
> And a gentle wife to rest with, and in my arms to fold,
> An Arabic book to study, a Norfolk cob to ride,
> And a house to live in shaded trees, and near to a river side;
> With such good things around me, and blessed with good health withal,
> Though I should live for a hundred years, for death I would not call."

George Borrow.

Two Recipes 〜 〜 〜 〜 〜

I. The Best Marrow-Bone Pye.

AFTER you have mixt the crusts of the best sort for pasts, and raised the coffin in such a manner as you please; you shall first in the bottome thereof lay a course of marrow of beef, mixt with currants; then upon it a lay of the soals of artichokes, after they have been boyled and are divided from the thistle; then cover them with marrow, currants, and great raisins, the stones pickt out; then lay a course of potatoes cut in thick slices, after they have been boiled soft, and are clean pilled; then cover them with marrow currants, great raisins, sugar, and cinnamon ; then lay a layer of candied eringo roots mixt very thick with the slices of dates ; then cover it with marrow, currants, great raisins, sugar, cinnamon, and dates, with a few Damask prunes, and so bake it ; and after it is bak't, pour into it, as long as it will receive it, white wine, rosewater, sugar, and cinnamon and vinegar mixt together, and candy all the cover with rosewater and sugar only, and so set it into the oven a little, and serve it forth.

II. An Excellent Sallet.

TAKE a good quantity of blancht almonds, and with your shredding knife cut them grossly ; then take as many raisins of the sun clean washt, and the stones pickt out, as many figs shred like the almonds, as many capers, twice so many olives, and as many currants as of all the rest, clean washt, a good handfull of the small tender leaves of red sage and spinage ; mixe all these well together with good store of sugar, and lay them in the bottome of a great dish ; then put unto them vinegar and oyl, and scrape more sugar over all ; then take oranges and lemmons, and paring away the outward pills, cut them into thin slices, then with those slices cover the sallet all over, which done, take the fine thin leaf of the red cole flower, and with them cover the oranges and lemmons all over ; then over those red leaves lay another course of old olives, and the slices of well pickled cucumbers, together with the

very inward heart of cabbage-lettuce cut into slices;
then adorn the sides of the dish, and the top of the
sallet, with more slices of lemmons and oranges, and
so serve it up.

Gervase Markham.

The Humble Feast ◦ ◦ ◦ ◦ ◦

NOW for a more humble Feast, or an ordinary
proportion which any good man may keep in
his family, for the entertainment of his true and
worthy friends, it must hold limitation with his
provision and the season of the year; for Summer
affords what Winter wants, and Winter is Master
of that which Summer can but with difficulty have.
It is good then for him that intends to Feast to
set down the full number of his full dishes, that is,
dishes of meat that are of substance, and not empty,
or for shew; and of these sixteen is a good proportion
for one course unto one messe, as thus, for example:
First, a shield of Brawn with mustard, Secondly, a
boyl'd Capon, Thirdly, a boyl'd piece of Beef, Fourthly,
a chine of Beef rosted, Fifthly, a Neat's tongue rosted,
Sixthly, a Pig rosted, Seventhly, Chewets bak'd,
Eighthly, a Goose rosted, Ninthly, a Swan rosted,
Tenthly, a Turkey rosted, the Eleventh, a Haunch
of Venison rosted, the Twelfth, a Pasty of Venison,
the Thirteenth, a Kid with a pudding in the belly,
the Fourteenth, an Olive-pye, the Fifteenth, a couple

of Capons, the Sixteenth, a Custard or Dousets. Now to these full dishes may be added Sallets, Fricases, Quelque choses, and devised paste, as many dishes more, which make the full service no less than two and thirty dishes, which is as much as can conveniently stand on one Table, and in one mess ; and after this manner you may proportion both your second and third Course, holding fulness in one half of the dishes, and shew in the other, which will be both frugall in the spender, contentment to the guests, and much pleasure and delight to the beholders.

Gervase Markham.

The Succedaneum

'TIS here ; this oval box well fill'd
    With best tobacco finely mill'd,
Beats all Anticyra's pretences
To disengage the encumbered senses.
"Oh ! nymph of Transatlantic fame,
Where'er thine haunt, whate'er thy name,
Whether reposing on the side
Of Oroonoquo's spacious tide,
Or listening with delight not small
To Niagara's distant fall,
'Tis thine to cherish and to feed
The pungent nose-refreshing weed,

Which, whether pulverised it gain
A shady passage to the brain,
Or whether, touch'd with fire, it rise
In circling eddies to the skies,
Does thought more quicken and refine
Than all the breath of all the Nine.
Forgive the bard, if bard he be,
Who once too wantonly made free
To touch with a satiric wipe
That symbol of thy power—the pipe ;
So may no blight invest thy plains,
And no unseasonable rains. . . .
And thou, secure from all alarms
Of thundering guns and glittering arms,
Rove unconfined beneath the shade
Thy wide-expanded leaves have made ;
So may thy victories increase
And fumigation never cease."

William Cowper.

Salvation Yeo's Testimony to Tobacco 〜 〜

AH sir, no lie, but a blessed truth, as I can tell,
who have ere now gone in the strength of
this weed three days and nights without eating ; and
therefore, sir, the Indians always carry it with them
on their war-parties : and no wonder ; for when all
things were made none was made better than this ;
to be a lone man's companion, a bachelor's friend,

a hungry man's food, a sad man's cordial, a wakeful man's sleep, and a chilly man's fire, sir; while for stanching of wounds, purging of rheum, and settling of the stomach, there's no herb like unto it under the canopy of heaven.

Charles Kingsley.

If I were King

IF I were King, my pipe should be premier.
   The skies of time and chance are seldom clear;
We would inform them all with azure weather.
Delight alone would need to shed a tear,
For dream and deed should war no more together.
Art should aspire, yet ugliness be dear;
Beauty, the shaft, should speed with wit for feather;
And love, sweet love, should never fall to sere,
      If I were King.

But politics should find no harbour near;
The Philistine should dread to slip his tether;
Tobacco should be duty free, and beer;
In fact, in room of this, the age of leather,
An age of gold all radiant should appear,
      If I were King.

W. E. Henley.

GARDEN AND ORCHARD

The idle life I lead
Is like a pleasant sleep,
Wherein I rest and heed
The dreams that by me sweep.

And still of all my dreams
In turn so swiftly past,
Each in its fancy seems
A nobler than the last.

And every eve I say,
Noting my step in bliss,
That I have known no day,
In all my life like this.

Robert Bridges.

But in the orchard is a place
    Where we may lie, and feel the fall
Of Apple-petals on our face,
    And drowsing hear the cuckoo's call.

The ring-dove's melancholy note,
    The blackbird's fluting, and the hum
Of bees above us, more remote,
    As slumber steals our senses. Come.

H. C. Beeching.

Nay, you shall see mine orchard, where, in an arbour, we will
eat a last year's pippin of my own graffing, with a dish of cara-
ways, and so forth :—come, cousin Silence ;—and then to bed.

Mr. Justice Shallow.

My Garden

A GARDEN is a lovesome thing, God wot!
  Rose plot,
  Fringed pool,
Ferned grot—
  The veriest school
  Of peace; and yet the fool
Contends that God is not—
Not God! in gardens! when the eve is cool?
  Nay, but I have a sign;
  'Tis very sure God walks in mine.
                        Thomas Edward Brown.

A Garden Song

H ERE, in this sequestered close
    Bloom the hyacinth and rose;
Here beside the modest stock
Flaunts the flaring hollyhock;
Here, without a pang, one sees
Ranks, conditions, and degrees.

All the seasons run their race
In this quiet resting-place ;
Peach, and apricot, and fig
Here will ripen, and grow big ;
Here is store and overplus,—
More had not Alcinous !

Here, in alleys cool and green,
Far ahead the thrush is seen ;
Here along the southern wall
Keeps the bee his festival ;
All is quiet else—afar
Sounds of toil and turmoil are.

Here be shadows large and long ;
Here be spaces meet for song ;
Grant, O garden-god, that I,
Now that none profane is nigh,—
Now that mood and moment please,
Find the fair Pierides !

Austin Dobson.

A Sunshiny Day   ◇   ◇   ◇   ◇   ◇

HERE is a glorious sunshiny day ; all the morning
I read about Nero in Tacitus, lying at full
length on a bench in the garden ; a nightingale
singing, and some red anemones eyeing the sun
manfully not far off. A funny mixture, all this ;

Nero and the delicacy of Spring; all very human, however. Then at half-past one lunch on Cambridge cream cheese; then a ride over hill and dale; then spudding up some weeds from the grass; and then, coming in, I sit down to write to you, my sister winding red worsted from the back of a chair, and the most delightful little girl in the world chattering incessantly. You think I live in Epicurean ease; but this happens to be a jolly day; one isn't always well, or tolerably good; the weather is not always clear, nor nightingales singing, nor Tacitus full of pleasant atrocity. But such as life is, I believe I have got hold of a good end of it.

Edward FitzGerald.

The Garden 〜 〜 〜 〜 〜

HOW vainly men themselves amaze,
    To win the palm, the oak, or bays,
And their incessant labours see
Crowned from some single herb, or tree,
Whose short and narrow-verged shade
Does prudently their toils upbraid,
While all the flowers and trees do close
To weave the garlands of repose!

Fair Quiet, have I found thee here,
And Innocence, thy sister dear?

Mistaken long, I sought you then
In busy companies of men.
Your sacred plants, if here below,
Only among the plants will grow ;
Society is all but rude
To this delicious solitude.

No white nor red was ever seen
So amorous as this lovely green.
Fond lovers, cruel as their flame,
Cut in these trees their mistress' name :
Little, alas ! they know or heed,
How far these beauties her exceed !
Fair trees ! where'er your barks I wound,
No name shall but your own be found.

When we have run our passion's heat,
Love hither makes his best retreat.
The gods, who mortal beauty chase,
Still in a tree did end their race ;
Apollo hunted Daphne so,
Only that she might laurel grow ;
And Pan did after Syrinx speed,
Not as a nymph, but for a reed.

What wondrous life is this I lead !
Ripe apples drop about my head ;
The luscious clusters of a vine
Upon my mouth do crush their wine ;

The nectarine, and curious peach,
Into my hands themselves do reach ;
Stumbling on melons, as I pass,
Ensnared with flowers, I fall on grass.

Meanwhile the mind, from pleasure less
Withdraws into its happiness ;—
The mind, that ocean where each kind
Does straight its own resemblance find ;
Yet it creates, transcending these,
Far other worlds, and other seas,
Annihilating all that's made
To a green thought in a green shade.

Here at the fountain's sliding foot,
Or at some fruit-tree's mossy root,
Casting the body's vest aside,
My soul into the boughs does glide :
There, like a bird, it sits and sings,
Then whets and claps its silver wings,
And, till prepared for longer flight,
Waves in its plumes the various light.

Such was that happy garden-state,
While man there walked without a mate :
After a place so pure and sweet,
What other help could yet be meet !
But 'twas beyond a mortal's share
To wander solitary there :
Two paradises are in one,
To live in paradise alone.

How well the skilful gardener drew
Of flowers, and herbs, this dial new,
Where, from above, the milder sun
Does through a fragrant zodiac run,
And, as it works, the industrious bee
Computes its time as well as we!
How could such sweet and wholesome hours
Be reckoned but with herbs and flowers?

Andrew Marvell.

Of Gardens

AND because the breath of flowers is far sweeter
in the air, where it comes and goes, like the
warbling of music, than in the hand, therefore nothing
is more fit for that delight, than to know what be the
flowers and plants that do best perfume the air. . . .
That which above all others yields the sweetest smell
in the air, is the violet ; especially the white double
violet, which comes twice a year, about the middle of
April, and about Bartholomew-tide. Next to that is
the musk rose ; then the strawberry leaves dying, with
a most excellent cordial smell ; then the flower of the
vines—it is a little dust, like the dust of a bent, which
grows upon the cluster, in the first coming forth ; then
sweet-brier ; then wallflowers, which are very delightful, to be set under a parlour, or lower chamber
window ; then pinks and gilliflowers, especially the

matted pink and clove gilliflower; then the flowers
of the lime-tree; then the honey-suckles, so they be
somewhat afar off. Of bean-flowers I speak not,
because they are field-flowers; but those which
perfume the air most delightfully, not passed by as
the rest, but being trodden upon and crushed, are
three; that is, burnet, wild thyme, and water mints.
Therefore you are to set whole alleys of them, to have
the pleasure when you walk or tread.

Francis Bacon.

Gardens ✑ ✑ ✑ ✑ ✑ ✑

I. Palace Gardens.

I AM filled with waters and gardens and groves and
vineyards, and the joyousness of the bordering
sea; and fisherman and farmer from different sides
stretch forth to me the pleasant gifts of sea and land:
and them who abide in me either a bird singing or the
sweet cry of the ferrymen lulls to rest.

Arabius.

II. The Garden God.

CALL me not him who comes from Libanus, O
stranger, who delights in the talk of young men
love-making by night; I am small and a rustic, born
of a neighbour nymph, and all my business is labour
of the garden; whence four garlands at the hands of

the four Seasons crown me from the beloved fruitful
threshing-floor.

Author unknown.
(J. W. Mackail's translation.)

Of an Orchard ～ ～ ～ ～ ～

G OOD is an Orchard, the Saint saith,
To meditate on life and death,
With a cool well, a hive of bees,
A hermit's grot below the trees.

Good is an Orchard : very good,
Though one should wear no monkish hood ;
Right good, when Spring awakes her flute,
And good in yellowing time of fruit.

Very good in the grass to lie
And see the network 'gainst the sky,
A living lace of blue and green,
And boughs that let the gold between.

The bees are types of souls that dwell
With honey in a quiet cell ;
The ripe fruit figures goldenly
The soul's perfection in God's eye.

Prayer and praise in a country home,
Honey and fruit : a man might come,
Fed on such meats, to walk abroad,
And in his Orchard talk with God.

Katharine Tynan Hinkson.

The Apple ✎ ✎ ✎ ✎ ✎ ✎

THE boy is indeed the true apple-eater, and is not to be questioned how he came by the fruit with which his pockets are filled. It belongs to him, and he may steal it if it cannot be had in any other way. His own juicy flesh craves the juicy flesh of the apple. Sap draws sap. His fruit-eating has little reference to the state of his appetite. Whether he be full of meat or empty of meat he wants the apple just the same. Before meal or after meal it never comes amiss. The farm-boy munches apples all day long. He has nests of them in the hay-mow, mellowing, to which he makes frequent visits. . . .

The apple is indeed the fruit of youth. As we grow old we crave apples less. It is an ominous sign. When you are ashamed to be seen eating them on the street; when you can carry them in your pocket and your hand not constantly find its way to them; when your neighbour has apples and you have none, and you make no nocturnal visits to his orchard; when your lunch-basket is without them and you can pass a winter's night by the fireside with no thought of the fruit at your elbow, then be assured you are no longer a boy either in heart or years.

John Burroughs.

I T was one of these delightfully irregular houses where you go up and down steps out of one room into another, and where you come upon more rooms when you think you have seen all there are, and where there is a bountiful provision of little halls and passages, and where you find still older cottage-rooms in unexpected places, with lattice windows and green growth pressing through them. Mine, which we entered first, was of this kind, with an up-and-down roof, that had more corners in it than I ever counted afterwards, and a chimney (there was a wood-fire on the hearth) paved all round with pure white tiles, in every one of which a bright miniature of the fire was blazing. Out of this room, you went down two steps into a charming little sitting-room, looking down upon a flower-garden, which room was henceforth to belong to Ada and me. Out of this you went up three steps, into Ada's bedroom, which had a fine broad window, commanding a beautiful view (we saw a great expanse of darkness lying underneath the stars), to which there was a hollow window-seat, in which, with a spring-lock, three dear Adas might have been lost at once. Out of this room, you passed into a little gallery, with which the other best rooms (only two) communicated, and so, by a little staircase of shallow steps, with a number of corner stairs in it, considering its length, down into the hall. But if, instead of going out at Ada's door, you came back into my room, and went out at the door by which you had entered it, and turned up a few crooked steps that branched off on an unexpected manner from the stairs, you lost yourself in passages, with mangles in them, and three-cornered tables, and a Native-Hindoo chair, which was also a sofa, a box, and a bedstead, and looked in every form, something between a bamboo skeleton and a great bird-cage, and had been brought from India nobody knew by whom or when. From these, you came on Richard's room, which was part library, part sitting-room, part bed-room, and seemed indeed a comfortable compound of many rooms. Out of that, you went straight, with a little interval of passage, to the plain room where Mr. Jarndyce slept, all the year round, with his window open, his bedstead without any furniture standing in the middle of the floor for more air, and his cold bath gaping for him in a smaller room adjoining. Out of that, you came into another passage, where there were back-stairs, and where you could hear the horses being rubbed down, outside the stable, and being told to Hold up, and Get over, as they slipped about very much on the uneven stones. Or you might, if you came out at another door (every room had at least two doors), go straight down to the hall again by half-a-dozen steps and a low archway, wondering how you got back there, or had ever got out of it.

The furniture, old-fashioned rather than old, like the house, was as pleasantly irregular Ada's sleeping-room was all flowers—in chintz and paper, in velvet, in needle-work, in the brocade of two stiff courtly chairs, which stood, each attended by a little page of a stool for greater state, on either side of the fire-place. Our sitting-room was green ; and had, framed and glazed, upon the walls, numbers of surprising and surprised birds, staring out of pictures at a real trout in a case, as brown and shining as if it had been served with gravy ; at the death of Captain Cook ; and at the whole process of preparing tea in China, as depicted by Chinese artists. In my room there were oval engravings of the months—ladies haymaking, in short waists, and large hats tied under the chin, for June—smooth-legged noblemen, pointing, with cocked hats, to village steeples, for October. Half-length portraits, in crayons, abounded all through the house ; but were so dispersed that I found the brother of a youthful officer of mine in the china-closet, and the grey old age of my pretty young bride, with a flower in her bodice, in the breakfast-room. As substitutes, I had four angels, of Queen Anne's reign, taking a complacent gentleman to heaven, in festoons, with some difficulty ; and a composition in needle-work, representing fruit, a kettle, and an alphabet. All the movables, from the wardrobes to the chairs and tables, hangings, glasses, even to the pincushions and scent-bottles on the dressing-tables, displayed the same quaint variety. They agreed in nothing but their perfect neatness, their display of the whitest linen, and their storing-up, wheresoever the existence of a drawer, small or large, rendered it possible, of quantities of rose-leaves and sweet lavender. Such, with its illuminated windows, softened here and **there** by shadows of curtains, shining out upon the star-light night ; with its light, and warmth, and comfort ; with its hospitable jingle, at a distance, of preparations for dinner ; with the face of its generous master brightening everything we saw ; and just wind enough without to sound a low accompaniment to everything we heard ; were our first impressions of Bleak House.

Charles Dickens.

With an Armchair ∽　　∽　　∽　　∽　　∽

ABOUT the oak that framed this chair of old,
　　The seasons danced their round ; delighted wings
Brought music to its boughs ; shy woodland things
Shared its broad roof, 'neath whose green glooms
　　grown bold,
Lovers, more shy than they, their secret told ;
The resurrection of a thousand springs
Swelled in its veins, and dim imaginings
Teased them, perchance, of life more manifold.
Such shall it know when its proud arms enclose
My Lady Goshawk, musing here at rest,
Careless of him who into exile goes,
Yet, while his gift by those fair limbs is prest,
Through some fine sympathy if nature knows
That, seas between us, she is still his guest.

J. R. Lowell.

OLD homes among the hills ! I love their gardens,
   Their old rock-fences, that our day inherits ;
Their doors, round which the great trees stand like
      wardens ;
Their paths, down which the shadows march like
      spirits ;
Broad doors and paths that reach bird-haunted
      gardens.

I see them gray among their ancient acres,
Severe of front, their gables lichen-sprinkled,
Like gentle-hearted, solitary Quakers,
Grave and religious, with kind faces wrinkled,
Serene among their memory-hallowed acres.

Their gardens, banked with roses and with lilies—
Those sweet aristocrats of all the flowers—
Where Springtime mints her gold in daffodillies,
And Autumn coins her marigolds in showers,
And all the hours are toilless as the lilies.

I love their orchards where the gay woodpecker
Flits, flashing o'er you, like a winged jewel ;
Their woods, whose floors of moss the squirrels
      checker
With half-hulled nuts ; and where, in cool renewal,
The wild brooks laugh, and raps the red woodpecker.

Old homes ! old hearts ! Upon my soul forever
Their peace and gladness lie like tears and laughter ;

Like love they touch me, through the years that sever,
With simple faith ; like friendship, draw me after
The dreamy patience that is theirs forever.

Madison Cawein.

A Country Sunday with Sir Roger de Coverley ∾

'Αθανάτους μὲν πρῶτα θεοὺς, νόμῳ ὡς διάκειται,
Τίμα—   *Pythag.*

First, in obedience to thy country's rites,
Worship th' immortal gods.

I AM always very well pleased with a country
Sunday, and think, if keeping holy the seventh
day were only a human institution, it would be the
best method that could have been thought of for the
polishing and civilising of mankind. It is certain the
country people would soon degenerate into a kind of
savages and barbarians were there not such frequent
returns of a stated time, in which the whole village
meet together with their best faces, and in their
cleanliest habits, to converse with one another upon
indifferent subjects, hear their duties explained to
them, and join together in adoration of the Supreme
Being. Sunday clears away the rust of the whole
week, not only as it refreshes in their minds the
notions of religion, but as it puts both the sexes upon
appearing in their most agreeable forms, and exerting
all such qualities as are apt to give them a figure in
the eye of the village. A country fellow distinguishes

himself as much in the churchyard, as a citizen does upon the 'Change, the whole parish-politics being generally discussed in that place either after sermon or before the bell rings.

My friend Sir Roger, being a good churchman, has beautified the inside of his church with several texts of his own choosing. He has likewise given a handsome pulpit cloth, and railed in the communion-table at his own expense. He has often told me that at his coming to his estate he found his parishioners very irregular; and that, in order to make them kneel and join in the responses, he gave every one of them a hassock and a common Prayer-book; and at the same time employed an itinerant singing-master, who goes about the country for that purpose, to instruct them rightly in the tunes of the Psalms; upon which they now very much value themselves, and indeed outdo most of the country churches that I have ever heard.

As Sir Roger is landlord to the whole congregation, he keeps them in very good order, and will suffer nobody to sleep in it besides himself; for if by chance he has been surprised into a short nap at sermon, upon recovering out of it he stands up and looks about him, and if he sees anybody else nodding, either wakes them himself or sends his servant to them. Several other of the old knight's particularities break out upon these occasions. Sometimes he will be lengthening out a verse in the singing Psalms half a minute after the rest of the congregation have done with it; sometimes when he is pleased with the matter of his devotion, he pronounces amen three or four times to the same prayer; and sometimes stands up when everybody else is upon their knees, to count the congregation, or see if any of his tenants are missing.

I was yesterday very much surprised to hear my old friend in the midst of the service calling out to one John Matthews to mind what he was about, and not disturb the congregation. This John Matthews, it seems, is remarkable for being an idle fellow, and at that time was kicking his heels for his diversion. This authority of the knight, though exerted in that odd manner which accompanies him in all circumstances of life, has a very good effect upon the parish, who are not polite enough to see anything ridiculous in his behaviour; besides that the general good sense and worthiness of his character make his friends observe these little singularities as foils that rather set off than blemish his good qualities.

As soon as the sermon is finished, nobody presumes to stir till Sir Roger is gone out of the church. The knight walks down from his seat in the chancel between a double row of his tenants that stand bowing to him on each side; and every now and then inquires how such a one's wife, or mother, or son, or father, do, whom he does not see in church; which is understood as a secret reprimand to the person that is absent.

The chaplain has often told me that upon a catechising day, when Sir Roger has been pleased with a boy that answers well, he has ordered a Bible to be given him next day for his encouragement; and sometimes accompanies it with a flitch of bacon to his mother. Sir Roger has likewise added five pounds a year to the clerk's place; and, that he may encourage the young fellows to make themselves perfect in the Church service, has promised, upon the death of the present incumbent, who is very old, to bestow it according to merit.

Joseph Addison.

MUSIC BENEATH A BRANCH

He [the poet] doth not only show you the way, but giveth so sweet a prospect into the way, as will entice any man to enter into it ; nay, he doth, as if your journey should lie through a fair vineyard, at the very first give you a cluster of grapes, that full of that taste you may long to pass farther. . . . He cometh to you with words set in delightful proportion . . . and with a tale, forsooth, he cometh unto you ; with a tale which holdeth children from play, and old men from the chimney-corner.

Sir Philip Sidney.

The Scholar-Gipsy ∽ ∽ ∽ ∽ ∽

GO, for they call you, Shepherd, from the hill;
  Go, Shepherd, and untie the wattled cotes!
  No longer leave thy wistful flock unfed,
Nor let thy bawling fellows rack their throats,
  Nor the cropp'd grasses shoot another head.
    But when the fields are still,
  And the tired men and dogs all gone to rest,
    And only the white sheep are sometimes seen
    Cross and recross the strips of moon-blanch'd
        green;
  Come, Shepherd, and again begin the quest.

Here, where the reaper was at work of late,
  In this high field's dark corner, where he leaves
    His coat, his basket, and his earthen cruse,
And in the sun all morning binds the sheaves,
    Then here, at noon, comes back his stores to use;
      Here will I sit and wait,
    While to my ear from uplands far away
      The bleating of the folded flocks is borne;
      With distant cries of reapers in the corn—
All the live murmur of a summer's day.

P   225

Screen'd is this nook o'er the high, half-reap'd field,
  And here till sun-down, Shepherd ! will I be.
    Through the thick corn the scarlet poppies peep
  And round green roots and yellowing stalks I see
    Pale blue convolvulus in tendrils creep ;
      And air-swept lindens yield
  Their scent, and rustle down their perfum'd showers
    Of bloom on the bent grass where I am laid,
    And bower me from the August sun with shade ;
  And the eye travels down to Oxford's towers :

And near me on the grass lies Glanvil's book—
  Come, let me read the oft-read tale again,
    The story of that Oxford scholar poor
  Of pregnant parts and quick inventive brain,
    Who, tir'd of knocking at Preferment's door,
      One summer morn forsook
  His friends, and went to learn the Gipsy-lore,
    And roam'd the world with that wild brotherhood,
    And came, as most men deem'd, to little good,
  But came to Oxford and his friends no more.

But once, years after, in the country lanes,
  Two scholars, whom at college erst he knew,
    Met him, and of his way of life enquir'd ;
  Whereat he answer'd, that the Gipsy crew,
    His mates, had arts to rule as they desir'd
      The workings of men's brains ;
  And they can bind them to what thoughts they will :
    "And I," he said, "the secret of their art,

When fully learn'd, will to the world impart ;
　　But it needs happy moments for this skill."

This said, he left them, and return'd no more,
　　But rumours hung about the country-side,
　　　That the lost Scholar long was seen to stray,
　　Seen by rare glimpses, pensive and tongue-tied,
　　　In hat of antique shape, and cloak of grey,
　　　　The same the Gipsies wore.
　　Shepherds had met him on the Hurst in spring ;
　　　At some lone alehouse in the Berkshire moors,
　　　On the warm ingle-bench, the smock-frock'd boors
　　Had found him seated at their entering,

But, mid their drink and clatter, he would fly :
　　And I myself seem half to know thy looks,
　　　And put the shepherds, Wanderer ! on thy trace ;
　　And boys who in lone wheatfields scare the rooks
　　　I ask if thou hast pass'd their quiet place ;
　　　　Or in my boat I lie
　　Moor'd to the cool bank in the summer heats,
　　　Mid wide grass meadows which the sunshine fills
　　　And watch the warm, green-muffled Cumner hills
　　And wonder if thou haunt'st their shy retreats.

For most, I know, thou lov'st retired ground !
　　Thee, at the ferry, Oxford riders blithe,
　　　Returning home on summer-nights, have met
　　Crossing the stripling Thames at Bab-lock-hithe,
　　　Trailing in the cool stream thy fingers wet,
　　　　As the slow punt swings round :

And leaning backwards in a pensive dream,
　　And fostering in thy lap a heap of flowers
　　Pluck'd in shy fields and distant woodland bowers,
And thine eyes resting on the moonlit stream.

And then they land, and thou art seen no more.
　　Maidens, who from the distant hamlets come
　　To dance around the Fyfield elm in May,
Oft through the darkening fields have seen thee
　　roam,
　　Or cross a stile into the public way.
　　　Oft thou hast given them store
Of flowers—the frail-leaf'd, white anemone—
　　Dark bluebells drench'd with dews of summer
　　eves—
　　And purple orchises with spotted leaves—
But none hath words she can report of thee.

And, above Godstow Bridge, when hay-time's here
　　In June, and many a scythe in sunshine flames,
　　Men who through those wide fields of breezy
　　grass
Where black-wing'd swallows haunt the glittering
　　Thames,
　　To bathe in the abandon'd lasher pass,
　　　Have often pass'd thee near
Sitting upon the river bank o'ergrown ;
　　Mark'd thine outlandish garb, thy figure spare,
　　Thy dark vague eyes, and soft abstracted air ;
But, when they came from bathing, thou wert gone !

At some lone homestead in the Cumner hills,
    Where at her open door the housewife darns,
        Thou hast been seen, or hanging on a gate
To watch the threshers in the mossy barns.
        Children, who early range these slopes and late
            For cresses from the rills,
Have known thee watching, all an April day,
    The springing pastures and the feeding kine ;
        And mark'd thee, when the stars come out and
            shine,
Through the long dewy grass move slow away.

In Autumn, on the skirts of Bagley Wood—
    Where most the Gipsies by the turf-edg'd way
        Pitch their smok'd tents, and every bush you see
With scarlet patches tagg'd and shreds of grey,
        Above the forest-ground call'd Thessaly—
            The blackbird, picking food,
Sees thee, nor stops his meal, nor fears at all ;
    So often has he known thee past him stray,
    Rapt, twirling in thy hand a wither'd spray,
And waiting for the spark from Heaven to fall.

And once, in winter, on the causeway chill
    Where home through flooded fields foot-travellers
            go,
        Have I not pass'd thee on the wooden bridge,
Wrapt in thy cloak and battling with the snow,
        Thy face towards Hinksey and its wintry ridge ?
            And thou hast climb'd the hill,

And gain'd the white brow of the Cumner range;
    Turn'd once to watch, while thick the snowflakes
        fall,
    The line of festal light in Christ-Church hall—
Then sought thy straw in some sequester'd grange.

But what—I dream! Two hundred years are flown
    Since first thy story ran through Oxford halls,
      And the grave Glanvil did the tale inscribe
    That thou wert wander'd from the studious walls
      To learn strange arts, and join a Gipsy-tribe;
        And thou from earth art gone
    Long since, and in some quiet churchyard laid—
      Some country-nook, where o'er thy unknown grave
      Tall grasses and white flowering nettles wave,
    Under a dark, red-fruited yew-tree's shade.

—No, no, thou hast not felt the lapse of hours!
    For what wears out the life of mortal men?
      'Tis that from change to change their being rolls;
    'Tis that repeated shocks, again, again,
      Exhaust the energy of strongest souls
        And numb the elastic powers.
    Till having us'd our nerves with bliss and teen,
      And tir'd upon a thousand schemes our wit,
      To the just-pausing Genius we remit
    Our worn-out life, and are—what we have been.

Thou hast not liv'd, why should'st thou perish, so?
    Thou hadst *one* aim, *one* business, *one* desire;
      Else wert thou long since number'd with the dead!

Else hadst thou spent, like other men, thy fire !
  The generations of thy peers are fled,
    And we ourselves shall go ;
But thou possessest an immortal lot,
  And we imagine thee exempt from age
  And living as thou liv'st on Glanvil's page,
Because thou hadst—what we, alas ! have not.

For early didst thou leave the world, with powers
  Fresh, undiverted to the world without,
    Firm to their mark, not spent on other things ;
  Free from the sick fatigue, the languid doubt,
    Which much to have tried, in much been baffled,
      brings.
        O Life unlike to ours !
Who fluctuate idly without term or scope,
  Of whom each strives, nor knows for what he
    strives,
  And each half lives a hundred different lives ;
Who wait like thee, but not, like thee, in hope.

Thou waitest for the spark from heaven ! and we
  Light half-believers of our casual creeds,
    Who never deeply felt, nor clearly will'd,
  Whose insight never has born fruit in deeds,
    Whose vague resolves never have been fulfill'd ;
      For whom each year we see
Breeds new beginnings, disappointments new ;
  Who hesitate and falter life away,
  And lose to-morrow the ground won to-day—
Ah ! do not we, Wanderer ! await it too ?

Yes, we await it, but it still delays,
  And then we suffer ! and amongst us One,
    Who most has suffer'd, takes dejectedly
His seat upon the intellectual throne ;
    And all his store of sad experience he
      Lays bare of wretched days ;
Tells us his misery's birth and growth and signs,
  And how the dying spark of hope was fed,
    And how the breast was sooth'd, and how the
      head,
And all his hourly varied anodynes.

This for our wisest : and we others pine,
  And wish the long unhappy dream would end,
    And waive all claim to bliss, and try to bear
With close-lipp'd Patience for our only friend,
    Sad Patience, too near neighbour to Despair—
      But none has hope like thine !
Thou through the fields and through the woods
      dost stray,
    Roaming the country-side, a truant boy,
    Nursing thy project in unclouded joy,
And every doubt long blown by time away.

O born in days when wits were fresh and clear,
  And life ran gaily as the sparkling Thames ;
    Before this strange disease of modern life,
With its sick hurry, its divided aims,
    Its head o'ertax'd, its palsied hearts, was rife--
      Fly hence, our contact fear !

Still fly, plunge deeper in the bowering wood !
　　Averse, as Dido did with gesture stern
　　From her false friend's approach in Hades turn,
Wave us away, and keep thy solitude !

Still nursing the unconquerable hope,
　　Still clutching the inviolable shade,
　　　With a free, onward impulse brushing through,
　　By night, the silver'd branches of the glade—
　　　Far on the forest skirts, where none pursue,
　　　　On some mild pastoral slope
　　Emerge, and resting on the moonlit pales
　　　Freshen thy flowers as in former years
　　　With dew, or listen with enchanted ears,
From the dark dingles, to the nightingales !

But fly our paths, our feverish contact fly !
　　For strong the infection of our mental strife,
　　　Which, though it gives no bliss, yet spoils for rest ;
　　And we should win thee from thy own fair life,
　　　Like us distracted, and like us unblest.
　　　　Soon, soon thy cheer would die,
　　Thy hopes grow timorous, and unfix'd thy powers,
　　　And thy clear aims be cross and shifting made ;
　　　And then thy glad perennial youth would fade,
Fade, and grow old at last, and die like ours.

Then fly our greetings, fly our speech and smiles !
　　—As some grave Tyrian trader from the sea,
　　　Descried at sunrise an emerging prow

Lifting the cool-hair'd creepers stealthily,
    The fringes of a southward-facing brow
        Among the Ægæan Isles ;
And saw the merry Grecian coaster come,
    Freighted with amber grapes, and Chian wine,
        Green, bursting figs, and tunnies steep'd in brine ;
And knew the intruders on his ancient home,

The young light-hearted Masters of the waves—
    And snatch'd his rudder, and shook out more
        sail ;
    And day and night held on indignantly
O'er the blue Midland waters with the gale,
    Betwixt the Syrtes and soft Sicily,
        To where the Atlantic raves
Outside the Western Straits ; and unbent sails
    There, where down cloudy cliffs, through sheets of
        foam,
    Shy traffickers, the dark Iberians come ;
And on the beach undid his corded bales.
                                        Matthew Arnold.

L'Allegro ∾ ∾ ∾ ∾ ∾ ∾

H ENCE, loathéd Melancholy,
    Of Cerberus and blackest Midnight born
In Stygian cave forlorn,
'Mongst horrid shapes, and shrieks, and sights unholy !

Find out some uncouth cell
  Where brooding Darkness spreads his jealous wings
And the night raven sings ;
  There, under ebon shades and low-browed rocks
As ragged as thy locks,
  In dark Cimmerian desert ever dwell.
  But come, thou goddess fair and free,
In heaven yclept Euphrosyne,
And by men heart-easing Mirth,
Whom lovely Venus, at a birth
With two sister Graces more,
To ivy-crowned Bacchus bore :
Or whether (as some sager sing)
The frolic wind that breathes the spring,
Zephyr, with Aurora playing
As he met her once a-Maying,
There, on beds of violets blue
And fresh-blown roses washed in dew,
Filled her with thee, a daughter fair,
So buxom, blithe, and debonair.
  Haste thee, nymph, and bring with thee
Jest, and youthful Jollity,
Quips, and Cranks, and wanton Wiles,
Nods, and Becks, and wreathéd Smiles,
Such as hang on Hebe's cheek
And love to live in dimple sleek ;
Sport that wrinkled Care derides,
And Laughter holding both his sides.
Come, and trip it, as you go
On the light fantastic toe ;

And in thy right hand lead with thee
The mountain nymph, sweet Liberty;
And, if I give thee honour due,
Mirth, admit me of thy crew,
To live with her, and live with thee,
In unreprovéd pleasures free :—
    To hear the lark begin his flight,
And, singing, startle the dull night,
From his watch-tower in the skies,
Till the dappled dawn doth rise;
Then to come, in spite of sorrow,
And at my window bid good-morrow,
Through the sweet-briar, or the vine,
Or the twisted eglantine,
While the cock, with lively din,
Scatters the rear of darkness thin,
And to the stack, or the barn-door,
Stoutly struts his dames before;
Oft listening how the hounds and horn
Cheerly rouse the slumbering morn,
From the side of some hoar hill,
Through the high wood echoing shrill;
Sometime walking, not unseen,
By hedgerow elms, on hillocks green,
Right against the eastern gate
Where the great sun begins his state
Robed in flames and amber light,
The clouds in thousand liveries dight,
While the ploughman, near at hand,
Whistles o'er the furrowed land,

And the milkmaid singeth blithe,
And the mower whets his scythe,
And every shepherd tells his tale
Under the hawthorn in the dale.

    Straight mine eye hath caught new pleasures,
Whilst the landscape round it measures :
Russet lawns, and fallows gray,
Where the nibbling flocks do stray ;
Mountains, on whose barren breast
The labouring clouds do often rest ;
Meadows trim, with daisies pied,
Shallow brooks, and rivers wide ;
Towers and battlements it sees
Bosomed high in tufted trees,
Where, perhaps, some beauty lies,
The cynosure of neighbouring eyes.

    Hard by, a cottage chimney smokes
From betwixt two agéd oaks,
Where Corydon and Thyrsis met,
Are at their savoury dinner set
Of herbs, and other country messes,
Which the neat-handed Phillis dresses,
And then in haste her bower she leaves,
With Thestylis to bind the sheaves ;
Or, if the earlier season lead,
To the tanned haycock in the mead.

    Sometimes, with secure delight,
The upland hamlets will invite,
When the merry bells ring round
And the jocund rebecks sound

To many a youth and many a maid
Dancing in the checkered shade,
And young and old come forth to play
On a sunshine holyday,
Till the livelong daylight fail :
Then to the spicy nut-brown ale,
With stories told of many a feat :
How fairy Mab the junkets eat ;
She was pinched, and pulled, she said ;
And he, by friar's lantern led,
Tells how the drudging goblin sweat
To earn his cream-bowl duly set,
When, in one night, ere glimpse of morn,
His shadowy flail hath threshed the corn
That ten day-labourers could not end ;
Then lies him down the lubber fiend,
And, stretched out all the chimney's length,
Basks at the fire his hairy strength,
And crop-full, out of doors he flings,
Ere the first cock his matin rings.
Thus done the tales, to bed they creep,
By whispering winds soon lulled asleep.
    Towered cities please us then,
And the busy hum of men,
Where throngs of knights and barons bold,
In weeds of peace, high triumphs hold,
With store of ladies, whose bright eyes
Rain influence, and judge the prize
Of wit or arms, while both contend
To win her grace whom all commend.

There let Hymen oft appear
In saffron robe, with taper clear,
And pomp, and feast, and revelry,
With mask and antique pageantry ;
Such sights as youthful poets dream
On summer eves by haunted stream.
Then to the well-trod stage anon,
If Jonson's learnéd sock be on,
Or sweetest Shakespeare, Fancy's child,
Warble his native wood-notes wild,
And ever, against eating cares,
Lap me in soft Lydian airs
Married to immortal verse,
Such as the meeting soul may pierce
In notes with many a winding bout
Of linkéd sweetness long drawn out,
With wanton heed and giddy cunning,
The melting voice through mazes running,
Untwisting all the chains that tie
The hidden soul of harmony ;
That Orpheus' self may heave his head,
From golden slumber on a bed
Of heaped Elysian flowers, and hear
Such strains as would have won the ear
Of Pluto to have quite set free
His half-regained Eurydice.
These delights if thou canst give,
Mirth, with thee I mean to live.

John Milton.

239

RARELY, rarely comest thou,
     Spirit of Delight !
Wherefore hast thou left me now
     Many a day and night ?
Many a weary night and day
'Tis since thou art fled away.

How shall ever one like me
     Win thee back again ?
With the joyous and the free
     Thou wilt scoff at pain.
Spirit false ! thou hast forgot
All but those who need thee not.

As a lizard with the shade
     Of a trembling leaf,
Thou with sorrow art dismayed ;
     Even the sighs of grief
Reproach thee, that thou art not near
And reproach thou wilt not hear.

Let me set my mournful ditty
     To a merry measure :
Thou wilt never come for pity,
     Thou wilt come for pleasure ;
Pity then will cut away
Those cruel wings, and thou wilt stay.

I love all that thou lovest,
    Spirit of Delight !
The fresh Earth in new leaves dressed,
    And the starry night,
Autumn evening, and the morn
When the golden mists are born.

I love snow, and all the forms
    Of the radiant frost ;
I love waves, and winds, and storms—
    Everything almost
Which is Nature's, and may be
Untainted by man's misery.

I love tranquil solitude,
    And such society
As is quiet, wise, and good ;
    Between thee and me
What difference ?   But thou dost possess
The things I seek, not love them less.

I love Love—though he has wings,
    And like light can flee ;
But above all other things,
    Spirit, I love thee—
Thou art love and life !   Oh, come,
Make once more my heart thy home !

                    Percy Bysshe Shelley

IN the highlands, in the country places,
    Where the old plain men have rosy faces,
And the young fair maidens
Quiet eyes ;
Where essential silence cheers and blesses,
And for ever in the hill-recesses
Her more lovely music
Broods and dies.

O to mount again where erst I haunted ;
Where the old red hills are bird-enchanted,
And the low green meadows
Bright with sward ;
And when even dies, the million-tinted,
And the night has come, and planets glinted,
Lo, the valley hollow
Lamp-bestarred !

O to dream, O to awake and wander
There, and with delight to take and render
Through the trance of silence
Quiet breath ;
Lo ! for there, among the flowers and grasses,
Only the mightier movement sounds and passes ;
Only winds and rivers,
Life and Death.

Robert Louis Stevenson.

BEHOLD her, single in the field,
    Yon solitary Highland Lass !
Reaping and singing by herself ;
Stop here, or gently pass !
Alone she cuts and binds the grain,
And sings a melancholy strain ;
O listen ! for the Vale profound
Is overflowing with the sound.

No Nightingale did ever chaunt
More welcome notes to weary bands
Of travellers in some shady haunt
Among Arabian sands :
A voice so thrilling ne'er was heard
In spring-time from a Cuckoo-bird,
Breaking the silence of the seas
Among the farthest Hebrides.

Will no one tell me what she sings ?—
Perhaps the plaintive numbers flow
For old, unhappy, far-off things,
And battles long ago :
Or is it some more humble lay,
Familiar matter of to-day ?
Some natural sorrow, loss, or pain,
That has been, and may be again ?

Whate'er the theme, the Maiden sang
As if her song could have no ending ;

I saw her singing at her work,
And o'er the sickle bending ;—
I listened, motionless and still ;
And, as I mounted up the hill,
The music in my heart I bore,
Long after it was heard no more.

William Wordsworth.

Ruth ∾ ∾ ∾ ∾ ∾ ∾

SHE stood breast high among the corn,
    Clasped by the golden light of morn,
Like the sweetheart of the sun,
Who many a glowing kiss had won.

On her cheek an autumn flush,
Deeply ripened ;—such a blush
In the midst of brown was born,
Like red poppies grown with corn.

Round her eyes her tresses fell,
Which were blackest none could tell,
But long lashes veiled a light,
That had else been all too bright.

And her hat, with shady brim
Made her tressy forehead dim ;
Thus she stood amid the stooks,
Praising God with sweetest looks :

Sure, I said, Heav'n did not mean,
Where I reap thou shouldst but glean ;
Lay thy sheaf adown and come,
Share my harvest and my home.

Thomas Hood.

Cadmus and Harmonia   ᔐ   ᔐ   ᔐ

FAR, far, from here,
    The Adriatic breaks in a warm bay
Among the green Illyrian hills ; and there
The sunshine in the happy glens is fair,
And by the sea, and in the brakes.
The grass is cool, the sea-side air
Buoyant and fresh, the mountain flowers
More virginal and sweet than ours.

And there, they say, two bright and aged Snakes,
Who once were Cadmus and Harmonia,
Bask in the glens or on the warm sea-shore,
In breathless quiet, after all their ills.
Nor do they see their country, nor the place
Where the Sphinx lived among the frowning hills,
Nor the unhappy palace of their race,
Nor Thebes, nor the Ismenus, any more.

There those two live, far in the Illyrian brakes.
They had stay'd long enough to see,

In Thebes, the billow of calamity
Over their own dear children roll'd,
Curse upon curse, pang upon pang,
For years, they sitting helpless in their home ;
A grey old man and woman ; yet of old
The gods had to their marriage come,
And at the banquet all the Muses sang.

Therefore they did not end their days
In sight of blood ; but were rapt, far away,
To where the west wind plays,
And murmurs of the Adriatic come
To those untrodden mountain-lawns ; and there
Placed safely in changed forms, the Pair
Wholly forget their first sad life, and home,
And all that Theban woe, and stray
For ever through the glens, placid and dumb.

Matthew Arnold.

Ode on a Grecian Urn

THOU still unravish'd bride of quietness,
    Thou foster-child of silence and slow time,
Sylvan historian, who canst thus express
    A flowery tale more sweetly than our rhyme :
What leaf-fring'd legend haunts about thy shape
    Of deities or mortals, or of both,
        In Tempé or the dales of Arcady ?

What men or gods are these? What maidens loth?
  What mad pursuit? What struggle to escape?
    What pipes and timbrels? What wild ecstasy?

Heard melodies are sweet, but those unheard
  Are sweeter; therefore, ye soft pipes, play on;
Not to the sensual ear, but, more endear'd,
  Pipe to the spirit ditties of no tone:
Fair youth, beneath the trees, thou canst not leave
  Thy song, nor ever can those trees be bare;
    Bold Lover, never, never canst thou kiss,
Though winning near the goal—yet, do not grieve;
  She cannot fade, though thou hast not thy bliss,
    For ever wilt thou love, and she be fair!

Ah, happy, happy boughs! that cannot shed
  Your leaves, nor ever bid the Spring adieu;
And, happy melodist, unwearièd,
  For ever piping songs for ever new;
More happy love! more happy, happy love!
  For ever warm and still to be enjoy'd,
    For ever panting, and for ever young;
All breathing human passion far above,
  That leaves a heart high-sorrowful and cloy'd,
    A burning forehead, and a parching tongue.

Who are these coming to the sacrifice?
  To what green altar, O mysterious priest,
Lead'st thou that heifer lowing at the skies,
  And all her silken flanks with garlands drest?

What little town by river or sea-shore,
  Or mountain-built with peaceful citadel,
    Is emptied of this folk, this pious morn?
And, little town, thy streets for evermore
  Will silent be; and not a soul to tell
    Why thou art desolate, can e'er return.

O Attic shape! Fair attitude! with brede
  Of marble men and maidens overwrought,
With forest branches and the trodden weed;
  Thou, silent form, dost tease us out of thought
As doth eternity: Cold Pastoral!
  When old age shall this generation waste,
    Thou shalt remain, in midst of other woe
Than ours, a friend to man, to whom thou say'st,
  "Beauty is truth, truth beauty,"—that is all
    Ye know on earth, and all ye need to know.

                                        John Keats.

The Lotus-Eaters ∽   ∽   ∽   ∽   ∽

"COURAGE!" he said, and pointed toward the
    land,
"This mounting wave will roll us shoreward soon."
In the afternoon they came unto a land
In which it seemed always afternoon.
All round the coast the languid air did swoon,
Breathing like one that hath a weary dream.
Full-faced above the valley stood the moon;

And like a downward smoke, the slender stream
Along the cliff to fall and pause and fall did seem.

A land of streams ! some, like a downward smoke,
Slow-dropping veils of thinnest lawn, did go ;
And some thro' wavering lights and shadows broke,
Rolling a slumbrous sheet of foam below.
They saw the gleaming river seaward flow
From the inner land : far off, three mountain-tops,
Three silent pinnacles of aged snow,
Stood sunset-flush'd : and, dew'd with showery drops,
Up-clomb the shadowy pine above the woven copse.

The charmed sunset linger'd low adown
In the red West : thro' mountain clefts the dale
Was seen far inland, and the yellow down
Border'd with palm, and many a winding vale
And meadow, set with slender galingale ;
A land where all things always seem'd the same !
And round about the keel with faces pale,
Dark faces pale against that rosy flame,
The mild-eyed melancholy Lotus-eaters came.

Branches they bore of that enchanted stem,
Laden with flower and fruit, whereof they gave
To each, but whoso did receive of them,
And taste, to him the gushing of the wave
Far far away did seem to mourn and rave
On alien shores ; and if his fellow spake,
His voice was thin, as voices from the grave ;

And deep-asleep he seem'd, yet all awake,
And music in his ears his beating heart did make.

They sat them down upon the yellow sand,
Between the sun and moon upon the shore ;
And sweet it was to dream of Fatherland,
Of child, and wife, and slave ; but evermore
Most weary seem'd the sea, weary the oar,
Weary the wandering fields of barren foam.
Then some one said, " We will return no more " ;
And all at once they sang, " Our island home
Is far beyond the wave ; we will no longer roam."

Alfred, Lord Tennyson.

The Forsaken Merman

COME, dear children, let us away ;
   Down and away below.
Now my brothers call from the bay ;
Now the great winds shorewards blow ;
Now the salt tides seawards flow ;
Now the wild white horses play,
Champ and chafe and toss in the spray.
   Children dear, let us away !
    This way, this way !

Call her once before you go.
   Call once yet.
In a voice that she will know :
   " Margaret !   Margaret !"

Children's voices should be dear
(Call once more) to a mother's ear :
Children's voices, wild with pain.
      Surely she will come again.
Call her once, and come away.
      This way, this way.
" Mother dear, we cannot stay."
The wild white horses foam and fret.
      Margaret !   Margaret !

Come, dear children, come away down.
      Call no more.
One last look at the white-walled town,
And the little grey church on the windy shore.
      Then come down.
She will not come though you call all day.
      Come away, come away.

Children dear, was it yesterday
We heard the sweet bells over the bay?
      In the caverns where we lay,
      Through the surf and through the swell.
The far-off sound of a silver bell?
Sand-strewn caverns, cool and deep,
Where the winds are all asleep ;
Where the spent lights quiver and gleam ;
Where the salt weed sways in the stream ;
Where the sea-beasts, ranged all round,
Feed in the ooze of their pasture-ground ;
Where the sea-snakes coil and twine,
Dry their mail and bask in the brine ;

Where great whales come sailing by,
Sail and sail, with unshut eye,
Round the world for ever and aye?
    When did music come this way?
    Children dear, was it yesterday?

    Children dear, was it yesterday
    (Call yet once) that she went away?
    Once she sate with you and me,
        On a red gold throne in the heart of the sea,
        And the youngest sate on her knee.
She combed its bright hair, and she tended it well,
When down swung the sound of the far-off bell.
She sighed, she looked up through the clear green
    sea.
She said : " I must go, for my kinsfolk pray
In the little grey church on the shore to-day.
'Twill be Easter-time in the world—ah me !
And I lose my poor soul, Merman, here with thee."
I said : " Go up, dear heart, through the waves ;
Say thy prayer, and come back to the kind sea-caves ! "
        She smiled, she went up through the surf in
            the bay.
            Children dear, was it yesterday?

    Children dear, were we long alone ?
" The sea grows stormy, the little ones moan ;
Long prayers," I said, " in the world they say.
Come," I said, and we rose through the surf in the
    bay.

We went up the beach, by the sandy down
Where the sea-stocks bloom, to the white-walled town.
Through the narrow paved streets, where all was still,
To the little grey church on the windy hill.
From the church came a murmur of folk at their
  prayers,
But we stood without in the cold blowing airs.
We climbed on the graves, on the stones, worn with
  rains,
And we gazed up the aisle through the small leaded
  panes.
   She sate by the pillar ; we saw her clear :
   " Margaret, hist ! come quick, we are here !
   Dear heart," I said, " we are long alone.
   The sea grows stormy, the little ones moan."
But, ah, she gave me never a look,
For her eyes were sealed to the holy book.
   " Loud prays the priest ; shut stands the door."
Come away, children, call no more !
Come away, come down, call no more !

   Down, down, down.
   Down to the depths of the sea.
She sits at her wheel in the humming town,
   Singing most joyfully.
Hark what she sings : " O joy, O joy,
For the humming street, and the child with its toy.
For the priest, and the bell, and the holy well.
   For the wheel where I spun,
   And the blessed light of the sun !"

And so she sings her fill,
Singing most joyfully,
Till the shuttle drops from her hand,
And the whizzing wheel stands still.
She steals to the window, and looks at the sand;
And over the sand at the sea;
And her eyes are set in a stare;
And anon there breaks a sigh,
And anon there drops a tear
From a sorrow-clouded eye,
And a heart sorrow-laden,
A long, long sigh
For the cold strange eyes of a little Mermaiden
And the gleam of her golden hair.

Come away, away, children.
Come, children, come down.
The hoarse wind blows colder;
Lights shine in the town.
She will start from her slumber
When gusts shake the door;
She will hear the winds howling,
Will hear the waves roar.
We shall see, while above us
The waves roar and whirl,
A ceiling of amber,
A pavement of pearl.
Singing : " Here came a mortal,
But faithless was she.

And alone dwell for ever
The kings of the sea."

But, children, at midnight,
When soft the winds blow,
When clear falls the moonlight ;
When spring-tides are low :
When sweet airs come seaward
From heaths starred with broom ;
And high rocks throw mildly
On the blanched sands a gloom :
Up the still, glistening beeches,
Up the creeks we will hie ;
Over banks of bright seaweed
The ebb-tide leaves dry.
We will gaze, from the sand-hills,
At the white, sleeping town ;
At the church on the hill-side—
        And then come back down,
Singing : " There dwells a loved one,
But cruel is she.
She left lonely for ever
The kings of the sea."

Matthew Arnold

Kubla Khan

I N Xanadu did Kubla Khan
   A stately pleasure-dome decree :
Where Alph, the sacred river, ran
Through caverns measureless to man
   Down to a sunless sea.
So twice five miles of fertile ground
With walls and towers were girdled round :
And there were gardens bright with sinuous rills
Where blossomed many an incense-bearing tree ;
And here were forests ancient as the hills,
Enfolding sunny spots of greenery.

   But O ! that deep romantic chasm which slanted
Down the green hill athwart a cedarn cover !
A savage place ! as holy and enchanted
As e'er beneath a waning moon was haunted
By woman wailing for her demon-lover !
And from this chasm, with ceaseless turmoil seeth-
   ing,
As if this Earth in fast thick pants were breathing,
A mighty fountain momently was forced :
Amid whose swift half-intermitted burst
Huge fragments vaulted like rebounding hail,
Or chaffy grain beneath the thresher's flail :
And mid these dancing rocks at once and ever
It flung up momently the sacred river.
Five miles meandering with a mazy motion
Through wood and dale the sacred river ran,

Then reached the caverns measureless to man,
And sank in tumult to a lifeless ocean:
And 'mid this tumult Kubla heard from far
Ancestral voices prophesying war!

The shadow of the dome of pleasure
Floated midway on the waves;
Where was heard the mingled measure
From the fountain and the caves.
It was a miracle of rare device,
A sunny pleasure-dome with caves of ice!
A damsel with a dulcimer
In a vision once I saw:
It was an Abyssinian maid,
And on her dulcimer she played,
Singing of Mount Abora.
Could I revive within me
Her symphony and song,
To such a deep delight 'twould win me
That with music loud and long,
I would build that dome in air,
That sunny dome! those caves of ice!
And all who heard should see them there,
And all should cry, Beware! Beware!
His flashing eyes, his floating hair!
Weave a circle round him thrice,
And close your eyes with holy dread,
For he on honey-dew hath fed,
And drunk the milk of Paradise.

Samuel Taylor Coleridge

YET once more, O ye laurels, and once more,
　　Ye myrtles brown, with ivy never sere,
I come, to pluck your berries harsh and crude,
And with forced fingers rude
Shatter your leaves before the mellowing year.
Bitter constraint and sad occasion dear
Compels me to disturb your season due :
For Lycidas is dead, dead ere his prime,
Young Lycidas, and hath not left his peer :
Who would not sing for Lycidas ?　He knew,
Himself to sing, and build the lofty rhyme.
He must not float upon his watery bier
Unwept, and welter to the parching wind
Without the meed of some melodious tear.

　Begin, then, sisters of the sacred well
That from beneath the seat of Jove doth spring .
Begin, and somewhat loudly sweep the string ;
Hence with denial vain, and coy excuse :
So may some gentle muse
With lucky words favour my destined urn,
And, as he passes, turn,
And bid fair peace be to my sable shroud.

　For we were nursed upon the self-same hill,
Fed the same flock, by fountain, shade, and rill.
Together both, ere the high lawns appeared
Under the opening eyelids of the morn,
We drove a-field, and both together heard
What time the grey-fly winds her sultry horn,

Battening our flocks with the fresh dews of night,
Oft till the star that rose at evening bright
Toward heaven's descent had sloped his westering
    wheel.
Meanwhile the rural ditties were not mute,
Tempered to the oaten flute ;
Rough satyrs danced, and fauns with cloven heel
From the glad sound would not be absent long :
And old Damœtas loved to hear our song.

    But, oh ! the heavy change, now thou art gone,
Now thou art gone and never must return !
Thee, Shepherd, thee the woods, and desert caves,
With wild thyme and the gadding vine o'ergrown,
And all their echoes, mourn :
The willows, and the hazel copses green,
Shall now no more be seen
Fanning their joyous leaves to thy soft lays.
As killing as the canker to the rose,
Or taint-worm to the weanling herds that graze,
Or frost to flowers that their gay wardrobe wear
When first the white-thorn blows ;
Such, Lycidas, thy loss to shepherd's ear.
    Where were ye, Nymphs, when the remorseless
    deep
Closed o'er the head of your loved Lycidas ?
For neither were ye playing on the steep
Where your old bards, the famous Druids, lie,
Nor on the shaggy top of Mona high,
Nor yet where Deva spreads her wizard stream :
Ah me ! I fondly dream,

Had ye been there : for what could that have done?
What could the Muse herself that Orpheus bore,
The Muse herself, for her enchanting son
Whom universal nature did lament,
When by the rout that made the hideous roar
His gory visage down the stream was sent,
Down the swift Hebrus to the Lesbian shore?

Alas! what boots it with incessant care
To tend the homely, slighted, shepherd's trade,
And strictly meditate the thankless Muse?
Were it not better done, as others use,
To sport with Amaryllis in the shade,
Or with the tangles of Neæra's hair?
Fame is the spur that the clear spirit doth raise
(That last infirmity of noble mind)
To scorn delights and live laborious days :
But the fair guerdon when we hope to find,
And think to burst out into sudden blaze,
Comes the blind Fury with the abhorred shears
And slits the thin-spun life. "But not the praise,"
Phœbus replied, and touched my trembling ears ;
"Fame is no plant that grows on mortal soil,
Nor in the glistening foil
Set off to the world, nor in broad rumour lies,
But lives and spreads aloft by those pure eyes
And perfect witness of all-judging Jove :
As he pronounces lastly on each deed,
Of so much fame in heaven expect thy meed."—

O fountain Arethuse, and thou honoured flood,
Smooth-sliding Mincius, crowned with vocal reeds,

That strain I heard was of a higher mood :
But now my oat proceeds,
And listens to the herald of the sea
That came in Neptune's plea ;
He asked the waves, and asked the felon winds,
What hard mishap hath doomed this gentle swain?
And questioned every gust, of rugged winds,
That blows from off each beakéd promontory :
They knew not of his story ;
And sage Hippotades their answer brings,
That not a blast was from his dungeon strayed,
The air was calm, and on the level brine
Sleek Panope with all her sisters played,
It was that fatal and perfidious bark,
Built in the eclipse, and rigged with curses dark,
That sunk so low that sacred head of thine.

    Next, Camus, reverend sire, went footing slow,
His mantle hairy, and his bonnet sedge
Inwrought with figures dim and on the edge
Like to that sanguine flower inscribed with woe.
"Ah ! who hath reft," quoth he, "my dearest
    pledge !"—
Last came, and last did go,
The pilot of the Galilean lake.
Two massy keys he bore, of metals twain,
The golden opes, the iron shuts amain,
He shook his mitred locks, and stern bespake ;
"How well could I have spared for thee, young
    swain,
Enow of such as, for their bellies' sake,

Creep, and intrude, and climb into the fold !
Of other care they little reckoning make
Than how to scramble at the shearers' feast
And shove away the worthy bidden guest ;
Blind mouths ! that scarce themselves know how to
    hold
A sheep-hook, or have learned aught else the least
That to the faithful herdsman's art belongs !
What recks it them ? What need they ? They are
    sped,
And, when they list, their lean and flashy songs
Grate on their scrannel pipes of wretched straw :
The hungry sheep look up, and are not fed,
But, swoln with wind and the rank mist they draw,
Rot inwardly, and foul contagion spread ;
Besides what the grim wolf, with privy paw,
Daily devours apace, and nothing said :
But that two-handed engine at the door
Stands ready to smite once, and smite no more.' —
    Return, Alpheus, the dread voice is past,
That shrunk thy streams ; return, Sicilian Muse,
And call the vales, and bid them hither cast
Their bells and flowerets of a thousand hues.
Ye valleys low, where the mild whispers use
Of shades, and wanton winds, and gushing brooks,
On whose fresh lap the swart star sparely looks,
Throw hither all your quaint enamelled eyes
That on the green turf suck the honeyed showers,
And purple all the ground with vernal flowers.
Bring the rathe primrose that forsaken dies,

The tufted crow-toe, and pale jessamine,
The white pink, and the pansy freaked with jet,
The glowing violet,
The musk-rose, and the well-attired woodbine,
With cowslips wan that hang the pensive head,
And every flower that sad embroidery wears ;
Bid amaranthus all his beauty shed,
And daffodillies fill their cups with tears,
To strew the laureate hearse where Lycid lies.
For so, to interpose a little ease,
Let our frail thoughts dally with false surmise :
Ah me ! whilst thee the shores and sounding seas
Wash far away, where'er thy bones are hurled,
Whether beyond the stormy Hebrides,
Where thou, perhaps under the whelming tide,
Visit'st the bottom of the monstrous world ;
Or whether thou, to our moist vows denied,
Sleep'st by the fable of Bellerus old,
Where the great vision of the guarded mount
Looks toward Namancos and Bayona's hold :
Look homeward, angel, now, and melt with ruth ;
And, O ye dolphins, waft the hapless youth.

Weep no more, woeful shepherds, weep no more
For Lycidas, your sorrow, is not dead,
Sunk though he be beneath the watery floor.
So sinks the day-star in the ocean-bed,
And yet anon repairs his drooping head,
And tricks his beams, and, with new spangled ore,
Flames in the forehead of the morning sky :
So Lycidas sunk low, but mounted high,

Through the dear might of Him that walked the
    waves,
Where, other groves and other streams along,
With nectar pure his oozy locks he laves,
And hears the unexpressive nuptial song
In the blest kingdoms meek of joy and love.
There entertain him all the saints above,
In solemn troops and sweet societies
That sing, and, singing, in their glory move,
And wipe the tears for ever from his eyes.
Now, Lycidas, the shepherds weep no more ;
Henceforth thou art the genius of the shore
In thy large recompense, and shalt be good
To all that wander in that perilous flood.

    Thus sang the uncouth swain to the oaks and
    rills,
While the still morn went out with sandals gray ;
He touched the tender stops of various quills,
With eager thought warbling his Doric lay :
And now the sun had stretched out all the hills,
And now was dropt into the western bay :
At last he rose, and twitched his mantle blue :
To-morrow to fresh woods and pastures new.

John Milton.

Ode on Intimations of Immortality from Recollections of Early Childhood ◡ ◡ ◡

> The Child is father of the Man ;
> And I could wish my days to be
> Bound each to each by natural piety.

I

THERE was a time when meadow, grove, and
    stream,
The earth, and every common sight,
    To me did seem
    Apparelled in celestial light,
The glory and the freshness of a dream.
It is not now as it hath been of yore ;—
    Turn wheresoe'er I may,
    By night or day,
The things which I have seen I now can see no more.

II

    The Rainbow comes and goes,
    And lovely is the Rose ;
    The Moon doth with delight
Look round her when the heavens are bare ;
    Waters on a starry night
    Are beautiful and fair ;
The sunshine is a glorious birth ;
But yet I know, where'er I go,
That there hath passed away a glory from the
    earth.

III

Now, while the Birds thus sing a joyous song,
    And while the young Lambs bound
      As to the tabor's sound,
To me alone there came a thought of grief :
A timely utterance gave that thought relief,
      And I again am strong.
The Cataracts blow their trumpets from the steep :
No more shall grief of mine the season wrong ;
I hear the Echoes through the mountains throng,
The Winds come to me from the fields of sleep,
      And all the earth is gay ;
        Land and Sea
      Give themselves up to jollity,
        And with the heart of May
      Doth every Beast keep holiday ;—
        Thou Child of Joy,
Shout round me, let me hear thy shouts, thou happy
    Shepherd-boy !

Ye blessèd Creatures, I have heard the call
    Ye to each other make ; I see
The heavens laugh with you in your jubilee ;
    My heart is at your festival,
    My head hath its coronal,
The fulness of your bliss, I feel—I feel it all.
    Oh evil day ! if I were sullen
    While Earth herself is adorning

This sweet May morning,
And the Children are culling
On every side,
In a thousand valleys far and wide,
Fresh flowers ; while the sun shines warm,
And the Babe leaps up on his Mother's arm :—
I hear, I hear, with joy I hear !
—But there's a Tree, of many, one,
A single Field which I have looked upon,
Both of them speak of something that is gone :
The Pansy at my feet
Doth the same tale repeat :
Whither is fled the visionary gleam ?
Where is it now, the glory and the dream ?

V

Our birth is but a sleep and a forgetting :
The Soul that rises with us, our life's Star
Hath had elsewhere its setting,
And cometh from afar :
Not in entire forgetfulness,
And not in utter nakedness,
But trailing clouds of glory do we come
From God, who is our home :
Heaven lies about us in our infancy !
Shades of the prison-house begin to close
Upon the growing Boy,
But he beholds the light, and whence it flows,
He sees it in his joy ;

The Youth, who daily farther from the East
  Must travel, still is Nature's Priest,
   And by the vision splendid
   Is on his way attended ;
At length the Man perceives it die away,
And fade into the light of common day.

VI

Earth fills her lap with pleasures of her own ;
Yearnings she hath in her own natural kind,
And even with something of a Mother's mind,
   And no unworthy aim,
  The homely Nurse doth all she can
To make her Foster-child, her Inmate Man,
   Forget the glories he hath known,
And that imperial palace whence he came.

VII

Behold the Child among his new-born blisses,
A six years' darling of a pigmy size !
See, where 'mid work of his own hand he lies,
Fretted by sallies of his Mother's kisses,
With light upon him from his Father's eyes !
See, at his feet, some little plan or chart,
Some fragment from his dream of human life,
Shaped by himself with newly-learned art ;
   A wedding or a festival,
   A mourning or a funeral ;

268

And this hath now his heart,
          And unto this he frames his song :
          Then will he fit his tongue
To dialogues of business, love, or strife :
          But it will not be long
          Ere this be thrown aside,
          And with new joy and pride
The little Actor cons another part ;
Filling from time to time his "humorous stage"
With all the Persons, down to palsied Age,
That Life brings with her in her equipage ;
          As if his whole vocation
          Were endless imitation.

VIII

Thou, whose exterior semblance doth belie
          Thy Soul's immensity ;
Thou best Philosopher, who yet dost keep
Thy heritage, thou Eye among the blind,
That, deaf and silent, read'st the eternal deep,
Haunted for ever by the eternal mind,—
          Mighty Prophet ! Seer blest !
          On whom those truths do rest,
Which we are toiling all our lives to find,
In darkness lost, the darkness of the grave ;
Thou, over whom thy Immortality
Broods like the Day, a master o'er a Slave,
A Presence which is not to be put by ;
Thou little Child, yet glorious in the might
Of heaven-born freedom on thy being's height,

Why with such earnest pains dost thou provoke
The years to bring the inevitable yoke,
Thus blindly with thy blessedness at strife?
Full soon thy Soul shall have her earthly freight,
And custom lie upon thee with a weight,
Heavy as frost, and deep almost as life!

IX

O joy! that in our embers
Is something that doth live,
That nature yet remembers
What was so fugitive!
The thought of our past years in me doth breed
Perpetual benediction : not indeed
For that which is most worthy to be blest ;
Delight and liberty, the simple creed
Of Childhood, whether busy or at rest,
With new-fledged hope still fluttering in his breast :—
Not for these I raise
The song of thanks and praise ;
But for those obstinate questionings
Of sense and outward things,
Fallings from us, vanishings ;
Blank misgivings of a Creature
Moving about in worlds not realised,
High instincts before which our mortal Nature
Did tremble like a guilty thing surprised :
But for those first affections,
Those shadowy recollections,
Which, be they what they may,

Are yet the fountain light of all our day,
Are yet a master light of all our seeing ;
    Uphold us, cherish, and have power to make
Our noisy years seem moments in the being
Of the eternal Silence : truths that wake,
        To perish never ;
Which neither listlessness, nor mad endeavour,
      Nor Man nor Boy,
Nor all that is at enmity with joy,
Can utterly abolish or destroy !
    Hence, in a season of calm weather,
      Though inland far we be,
Our Souls have sight of that immortal sea
      Which brought us hither,
      Can in a moment travel thither
And see the children sport upon the shore,
And hear the mighty waters rolling evermore.

X

Then sing, ye Birds, sing, sing a joyous song !
    And let the young Lambs bound
    As to the tabor's sound !
  We in thought will join your throng
    Ye that pipe and ye that play,
    Ye that through your hearts to-day
    Feel the gladness of the May !
What though the radiance which was once so bright
Be now for ever taken from my sight,
    Though nothing can bring back the hour
Of splendour in the grass, of glory in the flower ;

We will grieve not, rather find
Strength in what remains behind ;
In the primal sympathy
Which having been must ever be ;
In the soothing thoughts that spring
Out of human suffering ;
In the faith that looks through death
In years that bring the philosophic mind.

XI

And O, ye Fountains, Meadows, Hills, and Groves
Forebode not any severing of our loves !
Yet in my heart of hearts I feel your might ;
I only have relinquished one delight
To live beneath your more habitual sway.
I love the Brooks, which down their channels fret,
Even more than when I tripped lightly as they :
The innocent brightness of a new-born Day
      Is lovely yet ;
The Clouds that gather round the setting sun
Do take a sober colouring from an eye
That hath kept watch o'er man's mortality ;
Another race hath been, and other palms are won.
Thanks to the human heart by which we live,
Thanks to its tenderness, its joys, its fears,
To me the meanest flower that blows can give
Thoughts that do often lie too deep for tears.
               William Wordsworth.

THE SEA AND THE RIVER

i will go back to the great sweet mother,
    Mother and lover of men, the sea.
I will go down to her, I and none other,
    Close with her, kiss her and mix her with me ;
Cling to her, strive with her, hold her fast ;
O fair white mother, in days long past
Born without sister, born without brother,
    Set free my soul as thy soul is free.

                    Algernon Charles Swinburne.

As the stars come out, and the night-wind
    Brings up the stream
    Murmurs and scents of the infinite sea.

                    Matthew Arnold.

O to sail in a ship,
To leave this steady unendurable land,
To leave the tiresome sameness of the streets, the sidewalks
    and the houses,
To leave you, O you solid motionless land, and entering a ship.
To sail and sail and sail !

                    Walt Whitman.

The sea is in the splendid sun
    Plunging so careless and grand.
                    Duncan Campbell Scott.

The Brook ∽ ∽ ∽ ∽ ∽

I COME from haunts of coot and hern,
   I make a sudden sally,
And sparkle out among the fern,
   To bicker down a valley.

By thirty hills I hurry down,
   Or slip between the ridges,
By twenty thorps, a little town,
   And half a hundred bridges.

Till last by Philip's farm I flow
   To join the brimming river,
For men may come and men may go
   But I go on for ever.

I chatter over stony ways,
   In little sharps and trebles,
I bubble into eddying bays,
   I babble on the pebbles.

With many a curve my banks I fret
   By many a field and fallow,
And many a fairy foreland set
   With willow-weed and mallow.

I chatter, chatter, as I flow
    To join the brimming river,
For men may come and men may go,
    But I go on for ever.

I wind about, and in and out,
    With here a blossom sailing,
And here and there a lusty trout,
    And here and there a grayling,

And here and there a foamy flake
    Upon me, as I travel
With many a silvery waterbreak
    Above the golden gravel,

And draw them all along, and flow
    To join the brimming river,
For men may come and men may go,
    But I go on for ever.

I steal by lawns and grassy plots,
    I slide by hazel covers ;
I move the sweet forget-me-nots
    That grow for happy lovers.

I slip, I slide, I gloom, I glance,
    Among my skimming swallows ;
I make the netted sunbeam dance
    Against my sandy shallows.

I murmur under moon and stars
    In brambly wildernesses ;

I linger by my shingly bars ;
　　I loiter round my cresses ;

And out again I curve and flow
　　To join the brimming river,
For men may come and men may go,
　　But I go on for ever.

Alfred, Lord Tennyson.

The River and the Sea ✑　✑　✑　✑

ONE evening he asked the miller where the river
　　went.

"It goes down the valley," answered he, "and
turns a power of mills—six score mills, they say,
from here to Unterdeck—and it none the wearier
after all. And then it goes out into the lowlands,
and waters the great corn country, and runs through
a sight of fine cities (so they say) where kings live
all alone in great palaces, with a sentry walking up
and down before the door. And it goes under bridges
with stone men upon them, looking down and smiling
so curious at the water, and living folks leaning their
elbows on the wall and looking over too. And then
it goes on and on, and down through marshes and
sands, until at last it falls into the sea, where the
ships are that bring parrots and tobacco from the
Indies. Ay, it has a long trot before it as it goes
singing over our weir, bless its heart !"

"And what is the sea ?" asked Will.

"The sea!" cried the miller. "Lord help us all, it is the greatest thing God made! That is where all the water in the world runs down into a great salt lake. There it lies, as flat as my hand and as innocent-like as a child; but they do say when the wind blows it gets up into water-mountains bigger than any of ours, and swallows down great ships bigger than our mill, and makes such a roaring that you can hear it miles away upon the land. There are great fish in it five times bigger than a bull, and one old serpent as long as our river and as old as all the world, with whiskers like a man, and a crown of silver on her head."

R. L. Stevenson.

The Little Waves of Breffny

THE grand road from the mountain goes shining
    to the sea,
  And there is traffic in it, and many a horse and cart,
But the little roads of Cloonagh are dearer far to me,
  And the little roads of Cloonagh go rambling
    through my heart.

A great storm from the ocean goes shouting o'er the
    hill,
  And there is glory in it and terror on the wind,
But the haunted air of twilight is very strange and still,
  And the little winds of twilight are dearer to my
    mind.

The great waves of the Atlantic sweep storming on
  their way,
  Shining green and silver with the hidden herring
    shoal,
But the Little Waves of Breffny have drenched my
  heart in spray,
  And the Little Waves of Breffny go stumbling
    through my soul.

Eva Gore Booth.

Salt and Sunny Days

OH, silent glory of the summer day !
    How, then, we watched with glad and indolent
  eyes
The white-sailed ships dream on their shining way,
  Till, fading, they were mingled with the skies.
Have we not watched her, too, on nights that steep
  The soul in peace of moonlight, softly move
As a most passionate maiden, who in sleep
  Laughs low, and tosses in a dream of love ?

And when the heat broke up, and in its place,
  Came the strong, shouting days and nights, that
    run,
All white with stars, across the labouring ways
  Of billows warm with storm, instead of sun,
In gray and desolate twilights, when no feet
  Save ours might dare the shore, did we not come
Through winds that all in vain against us beat
  Until we had the warm sweet-smelling foam

Full in our faces, and the frantic wind
  Shrieked round us, and our cheeks grew numb,
    then warm,
Until we felt our souls, no more confined,
  Mix with the waves, and strain against the storm?
Oh! the immense, illimitable delight
  It is, to stand by some tempestuous bay,
What time the great sea waxes warm and white
  And beats and blinds the following wind with
    spray!

Philip Bourke Marston.

The Sea Gipsy

I AM fevered with the sunset,
  I am fretful with the bay,
For the wander-thirst is on me
And my soul is in Cathay.

There's a schooner in the offing,
With her topsails shot with fire,
And my heart has gone aboard her
For the Islands of Desire.

I must forth again to-morrow!
With the sunset I must be
Hull down on the trail of rapture
In the wonder of the Sea.

Richard Hovey.

Clancy's Song

OH, I love old Ocean's smile,
 I love old Ocean's frowning ;
I love old Ocean all the while—
 My prayer's for death by drowning.

J. B. Connolly.

Sailor's Song

TO sea, to sea ! The calm is o'er ;
 The wanton water leaps in sport,
And rattles down the pebbly shore ;
 The dolphin wheels, the sea-cows snort,
And unseen mermaids' pearly song
Comes bubbling up, the weeds among.
 Fling broad the sail, dip deep the oar :
 To sea, to sea ! the calm is o'er.

To sea, to sea ! our wide-winged bark
 Shall billowy cleave its sunny way,
And with its shadow, fleet and dark,
 Break the caved Tritons' azure day,
Like mighty eagle soaring light
O'er antelopes on Alpine height.
 The anchor heaves, the ship swings free,
 The sails swell full. To sea, to sea !

Thomas Lovell Beddoes.

I. Spring on the Coast.

NOW is the season for a ship to run through the gurgling water, and no longer does the sea gloom, fretted with gusty squalls, and now the swallow plasters her round houses under the eaves, and the soft leafage laughs in the meadows. Therefore wind up your soaked cables, O sailors, and weigh your hidden anchors from the harbours, and stretch the forestays to carry your well-woven sails. This I the son of Bromius bid you, Priapus of the Anchorage.

Antipater of Sidon.

II. Saved by Faith.

THEY call me the little one, and say I cannot go straight and fearless on a prosperous voyage like ships that sail out to sea; and I deny it not; I am a little boat, but to the sea all is equal; fortune, not size, makes the difference. Let another have the advantage in rudders; for some put their confidence in this and some in that, but may my salvation be of God.

Leonidas of Tarentum.

III. Worship in Spring.

OCEAN lies purple in calm; for no gale whitens the fretted waves with its ruffling breath, and no longer is the sea shattered round the rocks and sucked back again down towards the deep. West winds breathe, and the swallow twitters over the straw-glued chamber that she has built. Be of good cheer, O skilled in seafaring, whether thou sail to the Syrtis or the Sicilian shingle : only by the altars of Priapus of the Anchorage burn a scarus or ruddy wrasse.

Agathias.

IV. To the Gods of Harbour and Headland.

HARBOUR-GOD, do thou, O blessed one, send with a gentle breeze the outward-bound sail of Archelaus down smooth water even to the sea ; and thou who hast the point of the shore inward, keep the convoy that is bound for the Pythian shrine ; and thenceforward, if all we singers are in Phoebus' care, I will sail cheerily on with a fair-flowing west wind.

Antiphilus.

V. To Apollo of Leucas.

PHOEBUS who holdest the sheer steep of Leucas, far seen of mariners and washed by the Ionian sea, receive of sailors this mess of hand-kneaded barley bread and a libation mingled in a little cup, and the gleam of a brief-shining lamp that drinks with half-saturate mouth from a sparing oil-flask ; in recompence whereof be gracious, and send on their sails a favourable wind to run with them to the harbours of Actium.

Philippus.

VI. To the Gods of Sea and Weather.

O MELICERTA son of Ino, and thou, sea-green Leucothea, mistress of Ocean, deity that shieldest from harm, and choirs of the Nereïds, and waves, and thou Poseidon, and Thracian Zephyrus, gentlest of the winds, carry me propitiously, sped through the broad wave, safe to the sweet shore of the Peiraeus.

Philodemus.
(J. W. Mackail's translation.)

The Wander-Lovers ∽ ∽ ∽

D OWN the world with Marna !
That's the life for me !
Wandering with the wandering wind,
Vagabond and unconfined !
Roving with the roving rain
Its unboundaried domain !
Kith and kin of wander-kind,
Children of the sea !

Petrels of the sea-drift !
Swallows of the lea !
Arabs of the whole wide girth
Of the wind-encircled earth !
In all climes we pitch our tents,
Cronies of the elements
With the secret lords of birth
Intimate and free.

All the seaboard knows us
From Fundy to the Keys ;
Every bend and every creek
Of abundant Chesapeake ;
Ardise hills and Newport coves
And the far-off orange groves
Where Floridian oceans break,
Tropic tiger seas.

Down the world with Marna,
Tarrying there and here !
Just as much at home in Spain
As in Tangier or Touraine !
Shakespeare's Avon knows us well,
And the crags of Neufchâtel :
And the ancient Nile is fain
Of our coming near.

Down the world with Marna,
Daughter of the air !
Marna of the subtle grace,
And the vision in her face !
Moving in the measures trod
By the angels before God !
With her sky-blue eyes amaze
And her sea-blue hair !

Marna with the trees' life
In her veins a-stir !
Marna of the aspen heart
Where the sudden quivers start !

Quick-responsive, subtle, wild !
Artless as an artless child,
Spite of all her reach of art !
Oh, to roam with her !

Marna with the wind's will,
Daughter of the sea !
Marna of the quick disdain,
Starting at the dream of stain !
At a smile with love aglow,
At a frown a statued woe,
Standing pinnacled in pain
Till a kiss sets free !

Down the world with Marna,
Daughter of the fire !
Marna of the deathless hope
Still alert to win new scope
Where the wings of life may spread
For a flight unhazarded !
Dreamy of the speech to cope
With the heart's desire.

Marna of the far quest
After the divine !
Striving ever for some goal
Past the blunder-god's control !
Dreaming of potential years
When no day shall dawn in fears !
That's the Marna of my soul,
Wander-bride of mine !

Richard Hovey.

BUT the mere fact of its being a tramp ship gave us many comforts : we could cut about with the men and officers, stay in the wheel-house, discuss all manner of things, and really be a little at sea. And truly there is nothing else. I had literally forgotten what happiness was, and the full mind—full of external and physical things, not full of cares and labours and rot about a fellow's behaviour. My heart literally sang : I truly care for nothing so much as that.

R. L. Stevenson.

The Nantucketers

THE Nantucketer, he alone resides and riots on the sea ; he alone, in Bible language, goes down to it in ships ; to and fro ploughing it as his own special plantation. *There* is his home ; *there* lies his business, which a Noah's flood would not interrupt, though it overwhelmed all the millions in China. He lives on the sea, as prairie cocks in the prairie ; he hides among the waves, he climbs them as chamois hunters climb the Alps. For years he knows not the land ; so that when he comes to it at last, it smells like another world, more strangely than the moon would to an Englishman. With the landless gull, that at sunset folds her wings and is rocked to sleep between the billows ; so at nightfall, the Nantucketer, out of sight of land, furls his sails, and lays him to his rest, while under his very pillow rush herds of walruses and whales.

Herman Melville.

Philosophy ∽   ∽   ∽   ∽   ∽

M AN that is born of a woman
    Has very little time to live :
He comes up like a fore-topmast staysail
And down like a small flying jib.

Suffolk Sea Song.

THE REDDENING LEAF

Laden deep with fruity cluster,
  Then September, ripe and haie
Bees about his basket fluster,—
Laden deep with fruity cluster.
Skies have now a softer lustre;
  Barns resound to flap of flail.

Thou then, too, of woodlands lover,
  Dusk October, berry-stained;
Wailed about of parting plover,—
Thou then, too, of woodlands lover.
Fading now are copse and cover;
  Forests now are sere and waned.

Austin Dobson.

Lo! sweeten'd with the summer light,
The full juiced apple, waxing over-mellow,
Drops in a silent autumn night.

Alfred, Lord Tennyson.

The Departure of Summer ⌒ ⌒ ⌒

S UMMER is gone on swallows' wings,
    And Earth has buried all her flowers :
No more the lark, the linnet sings,
But Silence sits in faded bowers.
There is a shadow on the plain
Of Winter ere he comes again,—
There is in woods a solemn sound
Of hollow warnings whispered round,
As Echo in her deep recess
For once had turned a prophetess.
Shuddering Autumn stops to list,
And breathes his fear in sudden sighs,
With clouded face, and hazel eyes
That quench themselves, and hide in mist.

                                    T. Hood.

To Autumn ⌒ ⌒ ⌒ ⌒ ⌒

S EASON of mists and mellow fruitfulness,
    Close bosom-friend of the maturing sun ;
Conspiring with him how to load and bless

With fruit the vines that round the thatch-eaves
      run ;
To bend with apples the moss'd cottage-trees,
  And fill all fruit with ripeness to the core ;
    To swell the gourd, and plump the hazel shells
With a sweet kernel ; to set budding more,
  And still more, later flowers for the bees,
  Until they think warm days will never cease,
    For Summer has o'er-brimm'd their clammy cells.

Who hath not seen thee oft amid thy store?
  Sometimes whoever seeks abroad may find
Thee sitting careless on a granary floor,
  Thy hair soft-lifted by the winnowing wind ;
Or on a half-reap'd furrow sound asleep,
  Drows'd with the fume of poppies, while thy hook
    Spares the next swath and all its twined flowers :
And sometimes like a gleaner thou dost keep
  Steady thy laden head across a brook ;
  Or by a cyder-press, with patient look,
    Thou watchest the last oozings hours by hours.

Where are the songs of Spring? Ay, where are
      they?
  Think not of them, thou hast thy music too,—
While barred clouds bloom the soft-dying day,
  And touch the stubble-plains with rosy hue ;
Then in a wailful choir the small gnats mourn
  Among the river sallows, borne aloft
    Or sinking as the light wind lives or dies ;

And full-grown lambs loud bleat from hilly bourn ,
   Hedge-crickets sing ; and now with treble soft
The red-breast whistles from a garden-croft ;
   And gathering swallows twitter in the skies.

                      John Keats.

Sweet Fern

THE subtle power in perfume found
   Nor priest nor sibyl vainly learned ;
On Grecian shrine or Aztec mound
   No censer idly burned.

That power the old-time worships knew,
   The Corybantes' frenzied dance,
The Pythian priestess swooning through
   The wonderland of trance.

And Nature holds, in wood and field,
   Her thousand sunlit censers still ;
To spells of flower and shrub we yield
   Against or with our will.

I climbed a hill path strange and new
   With slow feet, pausing at each turn ;
A sudden waft of west wind blew
   The breath of the sweet fern.

That fragrance from my vision swept
   The alien landscape ; in its stead,

Up fairer hills or youth I stepped,
  As light of heart as tread.

I saw my boyhood's lakelet shine
  Once more through rifts of woodland shade ;
I knew my river's winding line
  By morning mist betrayed.

With me June's freshness, lapsing brook,
  Murmurs of leaf and bee, the call
Of birds, and one in voice and look
  In keeping with them all.

A fern beside the way we went
  She plucked, and smiling, held it up,
While from her hand the wild, sweet scent
  I drank as from a cup.

O potent witchery of smell !
  The dust-dry leaves to life return,
And she who plucked them owns the spell
  And lifts her ghostly fern.

Or sense or spirit ?   Who shall say
  What touch the chord of memory thrills ?
It passed, and left the August day
  Ablaze on lonely hills.

                    John Greenleaf Whittier.

THE copse ha' got his shiady boughs,
    Wi' blackbirds' evemen whissles ;
The hills ha' sheep upon ther brows,
    The zummerleäze ha' thissles.
The meäds be gay in grassy May,
    But O vrom hill to holler,
Let I look down upon a groun'
    O' carn a-turnen yoller.

An' pease da grow in tangled beds,
    An' beäns be sweet to snuff, O ;
The tiaper woats da bend ther heads,
    The barley's beard is rough, O ;
The turnip green is fresh between
    The carn in hill ar holler,
But I'd look down upon the groun'
    O' wheat a-turnen yoller.

'Tis merry when the brawny men
    Da come to reap it down, O,
Wher glossy red the poppy head
    'S among the sta'ks so brown, O ;
'Tis merry while the wheat's in hile
    Ar when, by hill ar holler,
The leäzers thick da stoop to pick
    The ears so ripe an' yoller.

William Barnès.

IF you would have your kennel for sweetness of cry, then you must compound it of some large dogs, that have deep solemn Mouthes, and are swift in spending, which must as it were bear the base in the consort; then a double number of roaring and loud ringing Mouthes, which must bear the counter tenor; then some hollow plain sweet Mouthes, which must bear the mean or middle part: and so with these three parts of musick you shall make your cry perfect: and herein you shall observe that these Hounds thus mixt, do run just and even together and not hang off loose from one another, which is the vilest sight that may be; and you shall understand, that this composition is best to be made of the swiftest and largest deep mouthed dog, the slowest middle siz'd dog, and the shortest legg'd slender dog. Amongst these you may cast in a couple or two small single beagles, which as small trebles may warble amongst them: the cry will be a great deal the more sweet. . . . If you would have your kennel for depth of mouth, then you shall compound it of the largest dogs which have the greatest mouths and deepest slews, such as your West Countrey, Che-shire and Lanca-shire dogs are, and to five or six base couple of mouths shall not add above two couple of counter tenors, as many means, and not above one couple of Roarers, which being heard but now and then, as at the opening or hitting of a scent, will give much sweetness to the solemnness and graveness of the cry, and the musick thereof will be much more delightfull to the ears of every beholder.

Gervase Markham.

The Find

YON sound's neither sheep-bell nor bark,
    They're running—they're running, Go hark!
The sport may be lost by a moment's delay ;
    So whip up the puppies and scurry away.
Dash down through the cover by dingle and dell.
There's a gate at the bottom—I know it full well ;
And they're running—they're running,
           Go hark !

They're running—they're running, Go hark !
One fence and we're out of the park ;
    Sit down in your saddles and race at the brook,
    Then smash at the bullfinch ; no time for a look ;
Leave cravens and skirters to dangle behind ;
He's away for the moors in the teeth of the wind,
And they're running—they're running,
           Go hark !

They're running—they're running, Go hark !
Let them run on and run till it's dark !

Well with them we are, and well with them we'll be,
   While there's wind in our horses and daylight
      to see :
Then shog along homeward, chat over the fight,
And hear in our dreams the sweet music all night
Of—They're running—they're running,
               Go hark !

Charles Kingsley.

NIGHT AND THE STARS

Hail, Twilight, sovereign of one peaceful hour !
Not dull art Thou as undiscerning Night ;
But studious only to remove from sight
Day's mutable distinctions.   Ancient Power !
Thus did the waters gleam, the mountains lower
To the rude Briton, when, in wolf-skin vest
Here roving wild, he laid him down to rest
On the bare rock, or through a leafy bower
Look'd ere his eyes were closed.   By him was seen
The self same vision which we now behold,
At thy meek bidding, shadowy Power, brought forth :
These mighty barriers, and the gulf between ;
The flood, the stars ;—a spectacle as old
As the beginning of the heavens and earth !

William Wordsworth.

The Dog-star and Aldebaran, pointing to the restless Pleiades,
were half way up the Southern sky, and between them hung
Orion, which gorgeous constellation never burnt more vividly
than now, as it swung itself forth above the rim of the landscape.   Castor and Pollux with their quiet shine were almost
on the meridian ; the barren and gloomy Square of Pegasus
was creeping round to the north-west ; far away through the
plantation, Vega sparkled like a lamp suspended amid the
leafless trees, and Cassiopeia's chair stood daintily poised on
the uppermost boughs.

" One o'clock," said Gabriel.

Thomas Hardy.

To the Evening Star ✿ ✿ ✿ ✿

THOU fair-haired Angel of the Evening,
  Now whilst the sun rests on the mountains, light
Thy bright torch of love—thy radiant crown
Put on, and smile upon our evening bed !
Smile on our loves ; and while thou drawest the
Blue curtains of the sky, scatter thy silver dew
On every flower that shuts its sweet eyes
In timely sleep.   Let thy West Wind sleep on
The lake ; speak silence with thy glimmering eyes
And wash the dusk with silver.—Soon, full soon,
Dost thou withdraw ; then the wolf rages wide,
And the lion glares through the dun forest,
The fleeces of our flocks are covered with
Thy sacred dew ; protect them with thine influence !

William Blake.

Evemen in the Village ✿ ✿ ✿ ✿

NOW the light o' the west is a-turn'd to gloom,
  An' the men be at huome vrom ground ;
An' the bells be a-zenden āl down the Coombe
A muoanen an' dyen sound.

301

An' the wind is still,
An' the house-dogs da bark,
An' the rooks be a-vled to the elems high an' dark,
An' the water da roar at mill.

An' out droo yander cottage's winder-piane
The light o' the candle da shoot,
An' young Jemmy the blacksmith is down the liane
A-playen his jarman-flute.
An' the miller's man
Da zit down at his ease
'Pon the girt wooden seat that is under the trees,
Wi' his pipe an' his cider can.

Tha' da zā that tis zom'hat in towns to zee
Fresh fiazen vrom day to day :
Tha' mid zee em var me, ef the two or dree
I da love should but smile an' stay.
Zoo gi'e me the sky,
An' the air an' the zun,
An' a huome in the dell wher the water da run,
An' there let me live an' die.

William Barnes.

Night ∽ ∽ ∽ ∽ ∽

THE sun descending in the west,
The evening star does shine ;
The birds are silent in their nest,
And I must seek for mine.

The moon, like a flower
In heaven's high bower,
With silent delight
Sits and smiles on the night.

Farewell, green fields and happy grove,
Where flocks have ta'en delight ;
Where lambs have nibbled, silent move
The feet of angels bright :
Unseen they pour blessing,
And joy without ceasing,
On each bud and blossom,
On each sleeping bosom.

They look in every thoughtiess nest,
Where birds are covered warm ;
They visit caves of every beast,
To keep them all from harm.
If they see any weeping
That should have been sleeping,
They pour sleep on their head,
And sit down by their bed.

When wolves and tigers howl for prey
They pitying stand and weep,
Seeking to drive their thirst away,
And keep them from the sheep.
But if they rush dreadful
The angels most heedful
Receive each mild spirit
New worlds to inherit.

And there the lion's ruddy eyes
Shall flow with tears of gold :
And pitying the tender cries,
And walking round the fold,
Saying : Wrath by His meekness,
And by His health sickness,
Are driven away
From our immortal day.

And now beside thee, bleating lamb,
I can lie down and sleep,
Or think on Him who bore thy name,
Graze after thee, and weep.
For, washed in life's river,
My bright mane for ever
Shall shine like the gold,
As I guard o'er the fold.

William Blake.

Invocation ～ ～ ～ ～ ～ ～

I AM he that walks with the tender and growing
night,
I call to the earth and sea half-hid by the night.
Press close, bare-bosomed night—press close, magnetic
nourishing night !
Night of south winds—night of the large few stars.
Still nodding night—mad naked summer night.

Smile, O voluptuous cool-breath'd earth!
Earth of the slumbering and liquid trees!
Earth of departed sunset—earth of the mountain
    misty-topt!
Earth of the vitreous pour of the full moon just tinged
    with blue!
Earth of shine and dark mottling the tide of the river!
Earth of the limpid grey of clouds brighter and clearer
    for my sake!
Far-swooping elbow'd earth—rich apple-blossom'd
    earth—
Smile, for your lover comes.

Walt Whitman.

To Night

S WIFTLY walk o'er the western wave,
        Spirit of Night!
Out of the misty eastern cave
Where, all the long and lone daylight,
Thou wovest dreams of joy and fear
Which make thee terrible and dear,
        Swift be thy flight!

Wrap thy form in a mantle grey,
        Star in-wrought,
Blind with thine hair the eyes of Day;
Kiss her until she be wearied out.

U   305

Then wander o'er city, and sea, and land,
Touching all with thine opiate wand—
          Come, long-sought !

When I arose and saw the dawn,
          I sighed for thee ;
When light rode high, and the dew was gone
And noon lay heavy on flower and tree,
And the weary Day turned to his rest,
Lingering like an unloved guest,
          I sighed for thee.

Thy brother Death came, and cried,
     "Would'st thou me ? "
Thy sweet child Sleep, the filmy-eyed,
     Murmured like a noontide bee,
"Shall I nestle near thy side ?
Would'st thou me ? "—And I replied,
          " No, not thee."

Death will come when thou art dead,
     Soon, too soon—
Sleep will come when thou art fled.
Of neither would I ask the boon
I ask of thee, belovèd Night—
Swift be thine approaching flight,
          Come soon, soon !

                    Percy Bysshe Shelley.

Species Aeternitatis

I KNOW that I am mortal and ephemeral; but
when I scan the multitudinous circling spirals of
the stars, no longer do I touch earth with my feet, but
sit with Zeus himself, and take my fill of the ambrosial
food of the gods.

Ptolemaeus.
(J. W. Mackail's translation.)

Bevis and the Stars

UP through the branches of the oak he saw Lyra,
the purest star in the heavens, white as whitest
and clearest light may be, gleaming at the zenith of
the pale blue dome. But just above the horizon
northwards there was a faint white light, the faintest
aurora, as if another moon was rising there.

Then the North Star, minute but clear—so small,
and yet chosen for the axle and focus of the sky,
instead of sun-like Sirius—the North Star always shone
just over the group of elms by the orchard. Summer
and winter, spring and autumn, it was always there,
always over the elms—whether they were reddening
with the buds and flowers of February, whether they
were dull green now in the heats of August, whether
they were yellow in October.

Dick and his team, whose waggon goes backwards,
swung round it like a stone in a sling whirled about

307

the shoulders.   Sometimes the tail of the Bear, where
Dick bestrides his second horse, hung down behind
the elms into the vapour of the horizon.   Sometimes
the Pointers were nearly overhead.   If they were
hidden by a cloud, the Lesser Bear gave a point ; or
you could draw a line through Cassiopeia, and tell the
North by her chair of stars. . . .

When the few leaves left on this young oak were
brown, and rustled in a frosty night, the massy shoulder
of Orion came heaving up through it—first one bright
star, then another ; then the gleaming girdle, and the
less definite scabbard ; then the great constellation
stretched across the east.   At the first sight of Orion's
shoulder Bevis always felt suddenly stronger, as if a
breath of the mighty hunter's had come down and
entered into him.

He stood upright ; his frame enlarged ; his instep
lifted him as he walked, as if he too could swing the
vast club and chase the lion from his lair.   The
sparkle of Orion's stars brought to him a remnant of
the immense vigour of the young world, the frosty air
braced his sinews, and power came into his arms.

As the constellation rose, so presently new vigour
too entered into the trees, the sap moved, the buds
thrust forth, the new leaf came, and the nightingale
travelling up from the south sang in the musical April
nights.   But this was when Orion was south, and
Sirius flared like a night-sun over the great oak at the
top of the Home Field.

Richard Jefferies.

NIGHT is a dead monotonous period under a
roof; but in the open world it passes lightly,
with its stars and dews and perfumes, and the hours
are marked by changes in the face of Nature. What
seems a kind of temporal death to people choked
between walls and curtains, is only a light and living
slumber to the man who sleeps a-field. All night
long he can hear Nature breathing deeply and freely;
even as she takes her rest she turns and smiles; and
there is one stirring hour unknown to those who
dwell in houses, when a wakeful influence goes abroad
over the sleeping hemisphere, and all the outdoor
world are on their feet. It is then that the cock
first crows, not this time to announce the dawn, but
like a cheerful watchman speeding the course of
night. Cattle awake on the meadows; sheep break
their fast on dewy hillsides, and change to a new lair
among the ferns; and houseless men, who have lain
down with the fowls, open their dim eyes and behold
the beauty of the night.

At what inaudible summons, at what gentle touch
of Nature, are all these sleepers thus recalled in the
same hour to life? Do the stars rain down an influence, or do we share some thrill of mother earth
below our resting bodies? Even shepherds and old
country-folk, who are the deepest read in these
arcana, have not a guess as to the means or purpose
of this nightly resurrection. Towards two in the

morning they declare the thing takes place; and neither know nor inquire further. And at least it is a pleasant incident. We are disturbed in our slumber only, like the luxurious *Montaigne*, "that we may the better and more sensibly relish it." We have a moment to look upon the stars. And there is a special pleasure for some minds in the reflection that we share the impulse with all out-door creatures in our neighbourhood, that we have escaped out of the *Bastille* of civilisation, and are become, for the time being, a mere kindly animal and a sheep of Nature's flock.

R. L. Stevenson.

To Sleep ᧖ ᧖ ᧖ ᧖ ᧖ ᧖

A FLOCK of sheep that leisurely pass by,
   One after one; the sound of rain, and bees
Murmuring; the fall of rivers, winds, and seas,
Smooth fields, white sheets of water, and pure sky.
I've thought of all by turns; and yet do lie
Sleepless; and soon the small bird's melodies
Must hear first utter'd from my orchard trees,
And the first cuckoo's melancholy cry.
Even thus last night, and two nights more, I lay
And could not win thee, Sleep! by any stealth:
So do not let me wear to-night away:
Without Thee what is all the morning's wealth?

Come, blessèd barrier between day and day,
Dear mother of fresh thoughts and joyous health !
William Wordsworth.

I Met at Eve   ∽   ∽   ∽   ∽

I MET at eve the Prince of Sleep,
   His was a still and lovely face ;
He wandered through a valley steep,
   Lovely in a lonely place.

His garb was grey of lavender,
About his brows a poppy-wreath
Burned like dim coals, and everywhere
   The air was sweeter for his breath.

His twilight feet no sandals wore,
His eyes shone faint in their own flame,
Fair moths that gloomed his steps before
   Seemed letters of his lovely name.

His house is in the mountain ways,
A phantom house of misty walls,
Whose golden flocks at evening graze,
   And witch the moon with muffled calls.

Upwelling from his shadowy springs
Sweet waters shake a trembling sound,
There flit the hoot-owl's silent wings,
   There hath his web the silkworm wound.

Dark in his pools clear visions lurk,
And rosy, as with morning buds,
Along his dales of broom and birk
    Dreams haunt his solitary woods.

I met at eve the Prince of Sleep,
His was a still and lovely face ;
He wandered through a valley steep,
    Lovely in a lonely place.

                    Walter Ramal.

A LITTLE COMPANY OF GOOD
COUNTRY PEOPLE

With the open air and a leisurely life,
   Homespun, and spaniels, and honey,
An eave-full of swallows, a sun-browned wife,
   He's never a thought for money.

                              T. Farquharson.

         Simplify, simplify !

                              H. D. Thoreau.

Who can Live in Heart so Glad ∾   ∾

WHO can live in heart so glad
  As the merry Country Lad !
Who, upon a fair green balk,
May, at pleasure, sit and walk ;
And, amid the azure skies,
See the morning sun arise !
While he hears, in every Spring,
How the birds do chirp and sing ;
Or, before the hounds in cry,
See the hare go stealing by ;
Or, along the shallow brook,
Angling with a baited hook,
See the fishes leap and play,
In a blessed sunny day ;
Or to hear the partridge call
Till she have her covey all ;
Or to see the subtle fox,
How the villain plies the box !
After feeding on his prey ;
How he closely sneaks away

Through the hedge, and down the furrow,
Till he gets into his burrow !
Then the bee to gather honey ;
And the little black-haired coney,
On a bank, for sunny place,
With her forefeet wash her face :
Are not these, with thousands moe
Than the Courts of Kings do know,
The true pleasing spirit's sights,
That may breed true love's delights ?

Nicolas Breton.

The Barefoot Boy

BLESSINGS on thee, little man,
    Barefoot boy, with cheek of tan !
With thy turned-up pantaloons,
And thy merry whistled tunes ;
With thy red lip, redder still
Kissed by strawberries on the hill ;
With the sunshine on thy face,
Through thy torn brim's jaunty grace ;
From my heart I give thee joy,—
I was once a barefoot boy.

    Prince thou art,—the grown-up man
Only is republican.
Let the million-dollared ride !
Barefoot, trudging at his side,

Thou hast more than he can buy
In the reach of ear and eye,—
Outward sunshine, inward joy :
Blessings on thee, barefoot boy

Oh for boyhood's painless play,
Sleep that wakes in laughing day,
Health that mocks the doctor's rules,
Knowledge never learned of schools.
Of the wild bee's morning chase,
Of the wild flower's time and place,
Flight of fowl and habitude
Of the tenants of the wood ;
How the tortoise bears his shell,
How the woodchuck digs his cell,
And the ground-mole sinks his well
How the robin feeds her young,
How the oriole's nest is hung ;
Where the whitest lilies blow,
Where the freshest berries grow,
Where the ground-nut trails its vine,
Where the wood-grape's clusters shine ;
Of the black wasp's cunning way,
Mason of his walls of clay,
And the architectural plans
Of gray hornet artisans !
For, eschewing books and tasks,
Nature answers all he asks ;
Hand in hand with her he walks,
Face to face with her he talks,

Part and parcel of her joy.—
Blessings on the barefoot boy!

Oh for boyhood's time of June,
Crowding years in one brief moon,
When all things I heard or saw,
Me, their master, waited for.
I was rich in flowers and trees,
Humming-birds and honey-bees ;
For my sport the squirrel played,
Plied the snouted mole his spade ;
For my taste the blackberry cone
Purpled over hedge and stone ;
Laughed the brook for my delight
Through the day and through the night,
Whispering at the garden wall,
Talked with me from fall to fall ;
Mine the sand-rimmed pickerel pond,
Mine the walnut slopes beyond,
Mine, on bending orchard trees,
Apples of Hesperides !
Still as my horizon grew,
Larger grew my riches too ;
All the world I saw or knew
Seemed a complex Chinese toy,
Fashioned for a barefoot boy.

Oh for festal dainties spread,
Like my bowl of milk and bread ;

Pewter spoon and bowl of wood,
On the door-stone, gray and rude !
O'er me, like a regal tent,
Cloudy ribbed, the sunset bent,
Purple-curtained, fringed with gold,
Looped in many a wind-swung fold ;
While for music came the play
Of the pied frogs' orchestra ;
And, to light the noisy choir,
Lit the fly his lamp of fire.
I was monarch : pomp and joy
Waited on the barefoot boy !

Cheerily, then, my little man,
Live and laugh, as boyhood can !
Though the flinty slopes be hard,
Stubble-speared the new-mown sward,
Every morn shall lead thee through
Fresh baptisms of the dew ;
Every evening from thy feet
Shall the cool wind kiss the heat :
All too soon these feet must hide
In the prison cells of pride,
Lose the freedom of the sod,
Like a colt's for work be shod,
Made to tread the mills of toil,
Up and down in ceaseless moil :
Happy if their track be found
Never on forbidden ground ;

Happy if they sink not in
Quick and treacherous sands of sin.
Ah! that thou couldst know thy joy,
Ere it passes, barefoot boy!

John Greenleaf Whittier.

A Fair and Happy Milkmaid

IS a country wench, that is so far from making herself beautiful by art, that one look of hers is able to put all face physic out of countenance. She knows a fair look is but a dumb orator to commend virtue, therefore minds it not. All her excellences stand in her so silently, as if they had stolen upon her without her knowledge. The lining of her apparel (which is herself) is far better than outsides of tissue; for though she be not arrayed in the spoil of the silkworm, she is decked in innocency, a far better wearing. She doth not, with lying long a-bed, spoil both her complexion and conditions; nature hath taught her too immoderate sleep is rust to the soul; she rises therefore with chanticleer, her dame's cock, and at night makes lamb her curfew. In milking a cow and straining the teats through her fingers, it seems that so sweet a milk-press makes the milk the sweeter or whiter; for never came almond glove or aromatic ointment off her palm to taint it. The golden ears of corn fall and kiss her feet when she reaps them, as if they wished to be bound and led prisoners by the same hand that felled them. Her breath is her own, which scents all the year long of June, like a new-made haycock. She makes her hand hard with labour, and her heart soft with pity; and when winter's evenings fall early (sitting at her merry wheel) she sings a defiance to the giddy wheel of fortune. She doth all things with so sweet a grace, it seems ignorance will not suffer her to do ill, because her mind is to do well. She bestows her year's wages at next fair; and, in choosing her garments, counts no bravery in the world like decency. The garden and beehive are all her physic and chirurgery, and she lives the longer for it. She dares go alone and unfold sheep in the night, and fears no manner of ill because she means none; yet, to say truth, she is never alone, for she is still accompanied with old songs, honest thoughts, and prayers, but short ones; yet they have their efficacy, in that they are not palled with ensuing idle cogitations. Lastly, her dreams are so chaste that she dare tell them: only a Friday's dream is all her superstition; that she conceals for fear of anger. Thus lives she, and all her care is that she may die in the spring-time, to have store of flowers stuck upon her winding-sheet.

Sir Thomas Overbury.

I BE the Shepherd o' the farm :
　　An' be so proud a-roven round
Wi' my long crook a-thirt my yarm,
　　As ef I wer a king a-crown'd.

An' I da bide al day among
　　The bleäten sheep, an' pitch ther vuold ;
An' when the evemen shiades be long
　　Da zee 'em al a-penn'd an' tuold.

An' I da zee the frisken lam's,
　　Wi' swingen tails and woolly lags,
A-playen roun' ther veeden dams,
　　An' pullen o' ther milky bags.

An' I, bezide a hawtharn tree,
　　Da zit upon the zunny down,
While shiades o' zummer clouds da vlee
　　Wi' silent flight along the groun'.

An' there, among the many cries
　　O' sheep an' lam's, my dog da pass
A zultry hour wi' blinken eyes,
　　An' nose a-stratch'd upon the grass.

But in a twinklen, at my word,
　　The shaggy rogue is up an' gone
Out roun' the sheep lik' any bird,
　　To do what he's a-zent upon.

An' wi' my zong, an' wi' my fife,
    An' wi' my hut o' turf an' hurdles,
I wou'den channge my shepherd's life
    To be a-miade a king o' wordles.

An' I da goo to washen pool,
    A-sousen auver head an' ears
The shaggy sheep, to cleän ther wool,
    An' miake 'em ready var the shears.

An' when the shearen time da come,
    I be at barn vrom dawn till dark,
Wher zome da catch the sheep, and zome
    Da mark ther zides wi' miaster's mark.

An' when the shearen's al a-done,
    Then we da eat, an' drink, an' zing
In miaster's kitchen, till the tun
    Wi' merry sounds da shiake an' ring.

I be the Shepherd o' the farm :
    An' be so proud a-roven round
Wi' my long crook a-thirt my yarm,
    As ef I were a king a-crown'd.

                   William Barnes.

The Shepherd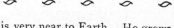

YOUR shepherd is very near to Earth. He grows up from her lap, he never quite leaves her bosom ; he is her foster-child. He may hear her heart-beats and drink of her tears. If she smiles he

knoweth why. He has listened and he knoweth.
She telleth him her secret thoughts; all the day
long he may lie close in her arms. No man so
proper for that sweet bed; no man may be so ready
to die and mingle with her.

Maurice Hewlett.
(*Pan and the Young Shepherd.*)

The Pretty Washermaiden ∽ ∽ ∽

THE pretty washermaiden,
  She washes on always !
And as she rubs, and as she wrings,
Her shapely body sways and springs
  As if to burst her stays.

Her cheek is rich and shining
  And brown as any egg,
And, when she dives into her tub
To duck the linen she's to scrub,
  She shows the neatest leg !

Her round arms white with lather,
  Her elbows fresh and red,
Her mouth the rosiest of buds,
Who would not risk a shower of suds
  To kiss her dainty head ?

W. E. Henley.

I KNEW a man, a common farmer, the father of
  five sons,
And in them the fathers of sons, and in them the
  fathers of sons.
This man was of wonderful vigour, calmness, beauty
  of person,
The shape of his head, the pale yellow and white
  of his hair and beard, the immeasurable meaning
  of his black eyes, the richness and breadth of his
  manners,
These I used to go and visit him to see, he was wise
  also,
He was six feet tall, he was over eighty years old,
  his sons were massive, clean, bearded, tan-faced,
  handsome,
They and his daughters loved him, all who saw him
  loved him,
They did not love him by allowance, they loved him
  with personal love,
He drank water only, the blood show'd like scarlet
  through the clear-brown of his face.
He was a frequent gunner and fisher, he sail'd his
  boat himself, he had a fine one presented to him
  by a ship-joiner, he had fowling-pieces presented
  to him by men that loved him,
When he went with his five sons and many grandsons
  to hunt or fish, you would pick him out as the
  most beautiful and vigorous of the gang,

You would wish long and long to be with him, you
would wish to sit by him in the boat that you and
he might touch each other.

Walt Whitman.

Tom Sueter ᴓ   ᴓ   ᴓ   ᴓ   ᴓ   ᴓ

WHAT a handful of steel-hearted soldiers are in
an important pass, such was Tom in keeping
the wicket. Nothing went by him; and for coolness
and nerve in this trying and responsible post, I never
saw his equal. As a proof of his quickness and
skill, I have numberless times seen him stump a
man out with Brett's tremendous bowling. Add to
this valuable accomplishment, he was one of the
manliest and most graceful of hitters. Few would
cut a ball harder at the point of the bat, and he was,
moreover, an excellent short runner. He had an eye
like an eagle—rapid and comprehensive. He was
the first who departed from the custom of the old
players before him, who deemed it a heresy to leave
the crease for the ball; he would get in at it, and hit
it straight off and straight on; and, egad! it went as
if it had been fired. As by the rules of our club, at
the trial-matches no man was allowed to get more
than thirty runs, he generally gained his number
earlier than any of them. I have seldom seen a
handsomer man than Tom Sueter, who measured
about five feet ten. As if, too, Dame Nature wished

to show at his birth a specimen of her prodigality, she gave him so amiable a disposition, that he was the pet of all the neighbourhood : so honourable a heart, that his word was never questioned by the gentlemen who associated with him ; and a voice, which for sweetness, power, and purity of tone (a tenor) would, with proper cultivation, have made him a handsome fortune. With what rapture have I hung upon his notes when he has given us a hunting song in the club-room after the day's practice was over. . . . Lear was a short man, of a fair complexion, well looking, and of a pleasing aspect. He had a sweet counter tenor voice. Many a treat have I had in hearing him and Sueter join in a glee at the "Bat and Ball" on Broad Halfpenny :

> I have been there, and still would go ;
> 'Twas like a little Heaven below !

John Nyren.

Uncle an' Aunt ∽ ∽ ∽ ∽

HOW happy uncle us'd to be
   O' zummer time, when aunt an' he
O' Zunday evemens, yarm in yarm,
Did walk about ther tiny farm,
While birds did zing, an' gnats did zwarm,
   Droo grass a'most above ther knees,
An' roun' by hedges an' by trees
   Wi' leafy boughs a-swayen.

His hat wer broad, his cuoat wer brown,
Wi' two long flaps a-hangèn down,
An' vrom his knee went down a blue
Knit stockèn to his buckled shoe,
An' aunt did pull her gown-tail droo
Her pocket-hole, to keep en neat,
As she mid walk, or teäke a seat
     By leafy boughs a-swayen.

An' vust they'd goo to zee their lots
O' pot-yarbs in the geärden plots ;
An' he, i'-maybe, gwain droo hatch
Would zee aunt's vowls upon a patch
O' zeeds, an' vow if he could catch
Em wi' his gun, they shoudden vlee
Noo mwore into their roostèn tree,
     Wi' leafy boughs a-swayen.

An' then vrom geärden tha did pass
Drough archet var to zee the grass,
An' if the blooth, so thick an' white,
Mid be at āl a-touch'd wi' blight,
An' uncle, happy at the zight,
Did guess what cider there mid be
In āl the archet, tree wi' tree,
     Wi' tutties all a-swayen.

An' then tha stump'd along vrom there
A-vield, to zee the cows an' meäre ;
An' she, when uncle come in zight,
Look'd up, an' prick'd her yers upright,

An' whicker'd out wi' āl her might ;
An' he, a-chucklèn, went to zee
The cows below the shiädy tree,
   Wi' leafy boughs a-swayen.

An' last ov āl, they went to know
How vast the grass in meäd did grow ;
An' then aunt zed 'twer time to goo
In huome, a-holdèn up her shoe
To show how wet 'e wer wi' dew.
An' zoo they toddled huome to rest,
Lik' culvers vlee-en to ther nest
   In leafy boughs a-swayen.

William Barnes.

Will Wimble

AS I was yesterday morning walking with Sir
Roger before his house, a country fellow
brought him a huge fish, which, he told him, Mr.
William Wimble had caught that very morning ; and
that he presented it with his service to him, and
intended to come and dine with him. At the same
time he delivered a letter, which my friend read to
me as soon as the messenger left him.

"SIR ROGER—I desire you to accept of a jack,
which is the best I have caught this season. I
intend to come and stay with you a week, and see

how the perch bite in the Black River. I observe
with some concern the last time I saw you upon the
bowling-green that your whip wanted a lash to it ; I
will bring half a dozen with me that I twisted last
week, which I hope will serve you all the time you
are in the country. I have not been out of the saddle
for six days last past, having been at Eton with Sir
John's eldest son. He takes to his learning hugely.—
I am, Sir, Your humble servant,

"WILL WIMBLE."

This extraordinary letter and message that accompanied it made me very curious to know the character
and quality of the gentleman who sent them, which
I found to be as follows :—Will Wimble is younger
brother to a baronet, and descended of the ancient
family of the Wimbles. He is now between forty
and fifty ; but being bred to no business and born to
no estate, he generally lives with his elder brother as
superintendent of his game. He hunts a pack of
dogs better than any man in the country, and is very
famous for finding out a hare. He is extremely well
versed in all the little handicrafts of an idle man.
He makes a May-fly to a miracle, and furnishes the
whole country with angle-rods. As he is a good-
natured, officious fellow, and very much esteemed
upon account of his family, he is a welcome guest at
every house, and keeps up a good correspondence
among all the gentlemen about him. He carries a
tulip root in his pocket from one to another, or

330

exchanges a puppy between a couple of friends that
live perhaps in the opposite sides of the county.
Will is a particular favourite of all the young heirs,
whom he frequently obliges with a net that he has
weaved, or a setting-dog that he has made himself.
He now and then presents a pair of garters of his
own knitting to their mothers or sisters, and raises
a great deal of mirth among them by inquiring as
often as he meets them "how they wear"! These
gentleman - like manufactures and obliging little
humours make Will the darling of the country.

Joseph Addison.

A Gentleman of the Old School ◦   ◦   ◦

HE lived in that past Georgian day,
　　When men were less inclined to say
That "Time is Gold," and overlay
　　　　With toil their pleasure ;
He held some land, and dwelt thereon,—
Where, I forget,—the house is gone ;
His Christian name, I think, was John,—
　　　　His surname, Leisure.

Reynolds has painted him,—a face
Filled with a fine, old-fashioned grace,
Fresh-coloured, frank, with ne'er a trace
　　　　Of trouble shaded ;

The eyes are blue, the hair is drest
In plainest way,—one hand is prest
Deep in a flapped canary vest,
      With buds brocaded.

He wears a brown old Brunswick coat,
With silver buttons,—round his throat,
A soft cravat ;—in all you note
      An elder fashion,—
A strangeness, which to us who shine
In shapely hats,—whose coats combine
All harmonies of hue and line,
      Inspires compassion.

He lived so long ago, you see !
Men were untravelled then, but we,
Like Ariel, post o'er land and sea
      With careless parting ;
He found it quite enough for him
To smoke his pipe in " garden trim,"
And watch, about the fish tank's brim,
      The swallows darting.

He liked the well-wheel's creaking tongue,—
He liked the thrush that stopped and sung,—
He liked the drone of flies among
      His netted peaches ;
He liked to watch the sunlight fall
Athwart his ivied orchard wall ;
Or pause to catch the cuckoo's call
      Beyond the beeches.

His were the times of Paint and Patch,
And yet no Ranelagh could match
The sober doves that round his thatch
        Spread tails and sidled ;
He liked their ruffling, puffed content,—
For him their drowsy wheelings meant
More than a Mall of Beaux that bent,
        Or Belles that bridled.

Not that, in truth, when life began
He shunned the flutter of the fan ;
He too had maybe " pinked his man "
        In Beauty's quarrel ;
But now his "fervent youth" had flown
Where lost things go ; and he was grown
As staid and slow-paced as his own
        Old hunter, Sorrel.

Yet still he loved the chase, and held
That no composer's score excelled
The merry horn, when Sweetlip swelled
        Its jovial riot ;
But most his measured words of praise
Caressed the angler's easy ways,—
His idly meditative days,—
        His rustic diet.

Not that his " meditating " rose
Beyond a sunny summer doze ;
He never troubled his repose
        With fruitless prying ;

But held, as law for high and low,
What God withholds no man can know,
And smiled away enquiry so,
            Without replying.

We read—alas, how much we read!—
The jumbled strifes of creed and creed
With endless controversies feed
            Our groaning tables ;
His books—and they sufficed him—were
Cotton's *Montaigne*, *The Grave* of Blair,
A "Walton"—much the worse for wear,
            And *Æsop's Fables*.

One more,—*The Bible*. Not that he
Had searched its page as deep as we ;
No sophistries could make him see
            Its slender credit ;
It may be that he could not count
The sires and sons to Jesse's fount,—
He liked the "Sermon on the Mount,"—
            And more, he read it.

Once he had loved, but failed to wed,
A red-cheeked lass who long was dead ;
His ways were far too slow, he said,
            To quite forget her ;
And still when time had turned him gray,
The earliest hawthorn buds in May
Would find his lingering feet astray,
            Where first he met her.

In Cœlo Quies heads the stone
On Leisure's grave,—now little known,
A tangle of wild-rose has grown
      So thick across it;
The "Benefactions" still declare
He left the clerk an elbow-chair,
And "12 Pence Yearly to Prepare
      A Christmas Posset."

Lie softly, Leisure! Doubtless you,
With too serene a conscience drew
Your easy breath, and slumbered through
      The gravest issue;
But we, to whom our age allows
Scarce space to wipe our weary brows,
Look down upon your narrow house,
      Old friend, and miss you!

Austin Dobson.

Mr. Hastings

MR. HASTINGS was low of stature, but very strong, and very active; of a ruddy complexion, with flaxen hair. His cloaths were always of green cloth. His house was of the old fashion; in the midst of a large park, well stocked with deer, rabbits, and fish-ponds. He had a long narrow bowling-green, in it; and used to play with round sand-bowls. Here too he had a banqueting-room built, like a stand, in a large tree. He kept all sorts of hounds, that ran buck, fox, hare, otter, and badger; and had hawks of all kinds, both long, and short winged. His great hall was commonly strewed with marrow-bones; and full of hawk-perches, hounds, spaniels, and terriers. The upper end of it was hung with fox-skins of this, and the last year's killing. Here, and there a pole-cat was intermixed; and hunter's poles in great abundance. The parlour was a large room, compleatly furnished in the same stile. On a broad hearth, paved with brick, lay some of the choicest terriers, hounds, and spaniels. One or two of the great chairs, had litters of cats in them, which were not to be disturbed. Of these three or four always attended him at dinner; and a little white wand lay by his trencher, to defend it, if they were too troublesome. In the windows, which were very large, lay his arrows, cross-bows, and other accoutrements. The corners of the room were filled with his best hunting, and hawking poles. His oister-table stood at the lower end of the room, which was in constant use twice a day, all the year round; for he never failed to eat oisters both at dinner, and supper; with which the neighbouring town of Pool supplied him. At the upper end of the room stood a small table with a double desk; one side of which held a church-bible; the other, the book of martyrs. On different tables in the room lay hawk's hoods; bells; old hats, with their crowns thrust in, full of pheasant eggs; tables;

dice ; cards ; and store of tobacco-pipes. At one end
of this room was a door, which opened into a closet ;
where stood bottles of strong beer, and wine ; which
never came out but in single glasses, which was the
rule of the house ; for he never exceeded himself ; nor
permitted others to exceed. Answering to this closet,
was a door into an old chapel ; which had been long
disused for devotion ; but in the pulpit, as the safest
place, was always to be found a cold chine of beef, a
venison-pasty, a gammon of bacon, or a great apple-
pye, with thick crust, well-baked. His table cost him
not much, tho' it was good to eat at. His sports
supplied all, but beef and mutton ; except on Fridays,
when he had the best of fish. He never wanted a
London pudding ; and he always sang it in with, *My
part lies therein-a.* He drank a glass or two of wine
at meals ; put syrup of gilly-flowers into his sack ; and
had always a tun-glass of small-beer standing by him,
which he often stirred about with rosemary. He lived
to be an hundred ; and never lost his eye-sight, nor
used spectacles. He got on horseback without help ;
and rode to the death of the stag, till he was past
fourscore.

William Gilpin.

I

EVERY village has its Jack, but no village ever
had quite so fine a Jack as ours :—
So picturesque,
Versatile,
Irresponsible,
Powerful,
Hedonistic,
And lovable a Jack as ours.

2

How Jack lived none knew, for he rarely did any
work.
True, he set night-lines for eels, and invariably caught
one,
Often two,
Sometimes three ;
While very occasionally he had a day's harvesting or
hay-making.
And yet he always found enough money for tobacco,
With a little over for beer, though he was no soaker.

3

Jack had a wife.
A soulless, savage woman she was, who disapproved
volubly of his idle ways.
But the only result was to make him stay out longer,
(Like Rip Van Winkle).

Jack had a big black beard, and a red shirt, which was
    made for another,
And no waistcoat.
His boots were somebody else's ;
He wore the Doctor's coat,
And the Vicar's trousers.
Personally, I gave him a hat, but it was too small.

5

Everybody liked Jack.
The Vicar liked him, although he never went to church.
Indeed, he was a cheerful Pagan, with no temptation
    to break more than the Eighth Commandment,
    and no ambition as a sinner.
The Curate liked him, although he had no simpering
    daughters.
The Doctor liked him, although he was never ill.
I liked him too — chiefly because of his perpetual
    good temper, and his intimacy with Nature, and
    his capacity for colouring cutties.
The girls liked him, because he brought them the first
    wild roses and the sweetest honeysuckle ;
Also, because he could flatter so outrageously.

6

But the boys loved him.
They followed him in little bands :
Jack was their hero.

And no wonder, for he could hit a running rabbit with a stone,

And cut them long, straight fishing - poles and equilateral catty forks ;

And he always knew of a fresh nest.

Besides, he could make a thousand things with his old pocket-knife.

7

How good he was at cricket too !

On the long evenings he would saunter to the green and watch the lads at play,

And by and by some one would offer him a few knocks.

Then the Doctor's coat would be carefully detached, and Jack would spit on his hands, and brandish the bat,

And away the ball would go, north and south and east and west,

And sometimes bang into the zenith.

For Jack has little science :

Upon each ball he made the same terrific and magnificent onslaught,

Whether half volley, or full pitch, or long hop, or leg break, or off break, or shooter, or yorker.

And when the stumps fell he would cheerfully set them up again, while his white teeth flashed in the recesses of his beard.

8

The only persons who were not conspicuously fond of
    Jack were his wife, and the schoolmaster, and the
    head-keeper.

The schoolmaster had an idea that if Jack were
    hanged there would be no more truants ;

His wife would attend the funeral without an extra-
    ordinary show of grief ;

And the head-keeper would mutter, "There's one
    poacher less."

Jack was quite as much a part of the village as the
    church spire ;

And if any of us lazied along by the river in the dusk
    of the evening—

Waving aside nebulæ of gnats,

Turning head quickly at the splash of a jumping fish,

Peering where the water chuckled over a vanishing
    water-rat—

And saw not Jack's familiar form bending over his
    lines,

And smelt not his vile shag,

We should feel a loneliness, a vague impression that
    something was wrong.

10

For ten years Jack was always the same,

Never growing older,

Or richer,
Or tidier,
Never knowing that we had a certain pride in possess-
    ing him.
Then there came a tempter with tales of easily-
    acquired wealth, and Jack went away in his
    company.

II

He has never come back,
And now the village is like a man who has lost an eye.
In the gloaming, no slouching figure, with colossal
    idleness in every line, leans against my garden
    wall, with prophecies of the morrow's weather ;
And those who reviled Jack most wonder now what it
    was they found fault with.
We feel our bereavement deeply.
The Vicar, I believe, would like to offer public prayer
    for the return of the wanderer.
And the Doctor, I know, is a little unhinged, and
    curing people out of pure absence of mind.
For my part, I have hope ; and the trousers I dis-
    carded last week will not be given away just yet.

E. V. Lucas.

The Vicar ◦   ◦   ◦   ◦   ◦

S OME years ago, ere time and taste
        Had turn'd our parish topsy-turvy,
When Darnel Park was Darnel Waste,
        And roads as little known as scurvy,

The man who lost his way, between
    St. Mary's Hill and Sandy Thicket,
Was always shown across the green,
    And guided to the Parson's wicket.

Back flew the bolt of lissom lath ;
    Fair Margaret, in her tidy kirtle,
Led the lorn traveller up the path,
    Through clean-clipt rows of box and myrtle ;
And Don and Sancho, Tramp and Tray,
    Upon the parlour steps collected,
Wagged all their tails, and seem'd to say,—
    " Our master knows you—you're expected."

Uprose the Reverend Dr. Brown,
    Uprose the Doctor's winsome marrow ;
The lady laid her knitting down,
    Her husband clasp'd his ponderous " Barrow " ;
Whate'er the stranger's caste or creed,
    Pundit or Papist, saint or sinner,
He found a stable for his steed,
    And welcome for himself, and dinner.

If, when he reach'd his journey's end,
    And warm'd himself in Court or College,
He had not gain'd an honest friend
    And twenty curious scraps of knowledge,—
If he departed as he came,
    With no new light on love or liquor,—
Good sooth, the traveller was to blame,
    And not the Vicarage, nor the Vicar.

His talk was like a stream, which runs
  With rapid change from rocks to roses :
It slipt from politics to puns,
  It passed from Mahomet to Moses ;
Beginning with the laws which keep
  The planets in their radiant courses,
And ending with some precept deep
  For dressing eels, or shoeing horses.

He was a shrewd and sound Divine,
  Of loud Dissent the mortal terror ;
And when, by dint of page and line,
  He 'stablished Truth, or startled Error,
The Baptist found him far too deep ;
  The Deist sigh'd with saving sorrow ;
And the lean Levite went to sleep,
  And dream'd of tasting pork to-morrow.

His sermon never said or show'd
  That Earth is foul, that Heaven is gracious,
Without refreshment on the road
  From Jerome, or from Athanasius :
And sure a righteous zeal inspired
  The hand and head that penn'd and plann'd them
For all who understood admired,
  And some who did not understand them.

He wrote, too, in a quiet way,
  Small treatises, and smaller verses,
And sage remarks on chalk and clay,
  And hints to noble Lords—and nurses ;

True histories of last year's ghost,
  Lines to a ringlet, or a turban,
And trifles for the *Morning Post*,
  And nothings for Sylvanus Urban.

He did not think all mischief fair,
  Although he had a knack of joking ;
He did not make himself a bear,
  Although he had a taste for smoking ;
And when religious sects ran mad,
  He held, in spite of all his learning,
That if a man's belief is bad,
  It will not be improved by burning.

And he was kind, and loved to sit
  In the low hut or garnish'd cottage,
And praise the farmer's homely wit,
  And share the widow's homelier pottage :
At his approach complaint grew mild ;
  And when his hand unbarr'd the shutter,
The clammy lips of fever smiled
  The welcome which they could not utter.

He always had a tale for me
  Of Julius Cæsar, or of Venus ;
From him I learnt the rule of three,
  Cat's cradle, leap-frog, and *Quæ genus :*
I used to singe his powder'd wig,
  To steal the staff he put such trust in,
And make the puppy dance a jig,
  When he began to quote Augustine.

Alack the change ! in vain I look
   For haunts in which my boyhood trifled,—
The level lawn, the trickling brook,
   The trees I climb'd, the beds I rifled :
The church is larger than before ;
   You reach it by a carriage entry ;
It holds three hundred people more,
   And pews are fitted up for gentry.

Sit in the Vicar's seat: you'll hear
   The doctrine of a gentle Johnian,
Whose hand is white, whose tone is clear,
   Whose phrase is very Ciceronian.
Where is the old man laid?—look down,
   And construe on the slab before you,
" *Hic jacet* GVLIELMVS BROWN,
   Vir nullâ non donandus lauru."

                    Winthrop Mackworth Praed.

The Fiddler of Dooney ✑   ✑   ✑   ✑

WHEN I play on my fiddle in Dooney,
   Folk dance like a wave of the sea ;
My cousin is priest in Kilvarnet,
   My brother in Maharabuiee.

I passed my brother and cousin :
   They read in their books of prayer ;
I read in my book of songs
   I bought at the Sligo fair.

When we cóme at the end of time,
    To Peter sitting in state,
He will smile on the three old spirits,
    But call me first through the gate ;

For the good are always the merry,
    Save by an evil chance,
And the merry love the fiddle,
    And the merry love to dance :

And when the folk there spy me,
    They will all come up to me,
With "Here is the fiddler of Dooney !"
    And dance like a wave of the sea.

W. B. Yeats.

Elegy on Captain Matthew Henderson, a gentleman who held the patent for his honours
immediately from Almighty God ∿ ∿

"Should the poor be flattered?"—*Shakespeare.*

O DEATH ! thou tyrant fell and bloody !
        The meikle devil wi' a woodie
Haurl thee hame to his black smiddie,
        O'er hurcheon hides,
And like stock-fish come o'er his studdie
        Wi' thy auld sides.

He's gane! he's gane! he's frae us torn,
The ae best fellow e'er was born!
Thee, Matthew, Nature's sel' shall mourn
                    By wood and wild,
Where, haply, pity strays forlorn,
                    Frae man exil'd!

Ye hills! near neebors o' the starns,
That proudly cock your cresting cairns!
Ye cliffs, the haunts of sailing yearns,
                    Where echo slumbers!
Come join, ye Nature's sturdiest bairns,
                    My wailing numbers!

Mourn, ilka grove the cushat kens!
Ye haz'lly shaws and briery dens!
Ye burnies, wimplin' down your glens,
                    Wi' toddlin' din,
Or foaming strang, wi' hasty stens,
                    Frae lin to lin!

Mourn, little harebells o'er the lea;
Ye stately foxgloves fair to see;
Ye woodbines, hanging bonnilie
                    In scented bow'rs;
Ye roses on your thorny tree,
                    The first o' flow'rs.

At dawn, when ev'ry grassy blade
Droops with a diamond at its head,

At ev'n, when beans their fragrance shed,
        I' th' rustling gale,
Ye maukins whiddin thro' the glade,
        Come join my wail.

Mourn, ye wee songsters o' the wood ;
Ye grouse that crap the heather bud ;
Ye curlews calling thro' a clud ;
        Ye whistling plover ;
An' mourn ye whirring paitrick brood !—
        He's gane for ever.

Mourn, sooty coots, and speckled teals ;
Ye fisher herons, watching eels ;
Ye duck and drake, wi' airy wheels
        Circling the lake ;
Ye bitterns, till the quagmire reels,
        Rair for his sake.

Mourn, clam'ring craiks at close o' day,
'Mang fields o' flowering clover gay ;
And when ye wing your annual way
        Frae our cauld shore,
Tell thae far warlds, wha lies in clay,
        Wham we deplore.

Ye houlets, frae your ivy bow'r,
In some auld tree, or eldritch tow'r,
What time the moon, wi' silent glow'r,
        Sets up her horn,
Wail thro' the dreary midnight hour
        Till waukrife morn !

O, rivers, forests, hills, and plains!
Oft have ye heard my canty strains
But now, what else for me remains
        But tales of woe?
And frae my een the drapping rains
        Maun ever flow.

Mourn, spring, thou darling of the year
Ilk cowslip cup shall kep a tear:
Thou, simmer, while each corny spear
        Shoots up its head,
Thy gay, green, flow'ry tresses shear
        For him that's dead!

Thou, autumn, wi' thy yellow hair,
In grief thy sallow mantle tear:
Thou, winter, hurling thro' the air
        The roaring blast,
Wide o'er the naked world declare,
        The worth we've lost!

Mourn him, thou sun, great source of light!
Mourn, empress of the silent night!
And you, ye twinkling starnies bright,
        My Matthew mourn!
For through your orbs he's ta'en his flight,
        Ne'er to return.

Oh, Henderson! the man—the brother!
And art thou gone, and gone for ever?

And hast thou crost that unknown river,
        Life's dreary bound?
Like thee, where shall I find another
        The world around?

Go to your sculptur'd tombs, ye great,
In a' the tinsel trash o' state!
But by thy honest turf I'll wait,
        Thou man of worth!
And weep the ae best fellow's fate
        E'er lay in earth.

THE EPITAPH

Stop, passenger!—my story's brief,
    And truth I shall relate, man;
I tell nae common tale o' grief—
    For Matthew was a great man.

If thou uncommon merit hast,
    Yet spurn'd at fortune's door, man.
A look of pity hither cast—
    For Matthew was a poor man.

If thou a noble sodger art,
    That passest by this grave, man,
There moulders here a gallant heart—
    For Matthew was a brave man.

If thou on men, their works and ways,
    Canst throw uncommon light, man,
Here lies wha weel had won thy praise—
    For Matthew was a bright man.

If thou at friendship's sacred ca'
  Wad life itself resign, man,
Thy sympathetic tear maun fa'—
  For Matthew was a kind man !

If thou art staunch without a stain,
  Like the unchanging blue, man,
This was a kinsman o' thy ain—
  For Matthew was a true man.

If thou hast wit, and fun, and fire,
  And ne'er guid wine did fear, man,
This was thy billie, dam, and sire--
  For Matthew was a queer man.

If ony whiggish whingin sot,
  To blame poor Matthew dare, man
May dool and sorrow be his lot !
  For Matthew was a rare man.

But now his radiant course is run,
  For Matthew's course was bright,
His soul was like the glorious sun,
  A matchless heav'nly light !

                                    Robert Burns.

A HANDFUL OF PHILOSOPHY

SANCHO PANZA'S PROVERBS

There is still sun on the wall.
It requires a long time to know any one.
All sorrows are bearable if there is bread.
He who does not rise with the sun does not enjoy the day.
Every one is as God made him, and very often worse.
Until death, all is life.
Praying to God and hammering away.

———

The world is too much with us ; late and soon,
Getting and spending, we lay waste our powers :
Little we see in Nature that is ours ;
We have given our hearts away, a sordid boon !
This sea that bares her bosom to the moon ;
The winds that will be howling at all hours,
And are up-gathered now like sleeping flowers ;
For this, for every thing, we are out of tune ;
It moves us not.—Great God ! I'd rather be
A Pagan suckled in a creed outworn ;
So might I, standing on this pleasant lea,
Have glimpses that would make me less forlorn ;
Have sight of Proteus rising from the sea ;
Or hear old Triton blow his wreathèd horn.

William Wordsworth

Content ✑ ✑ ✑ ✑ ✑ ✑

A RT thou poor, yet hast thou golden slumbers?
   O sweet content!
Art thou rich, yet is thy mind perplexéd?
   O punishment!
Dost thou laugh to see how fools are vexéd
To add to golden numbers, golden numbers?
O sweet content! O sweet, O sweet content!

 Work apace, apace, apace, apace;
 Hence labour bears a lovely face;
Then hey nonny nonny, hey nonny nonny!

Canst drink the waters of the crispéd spring?
   O sweet content!
Swimm'st thou in wealth, yet sink'st in thine own tears?
   O punishment!
Then he that patiently want's burden bears
No burden bears, but is a king, a king!
O sweet content! O sweet, O sweet content!

Work apace, apace, apace, apace ;
Honest labour bears a lovely face ;
Then hey nonny nonny, hey nonny nonny !
Thomas Dekker.

Henry VI.'s Pastoral Wish

OH God ! methinks it were a happy life
    To be no better than a homely swain,
To sit upon a hill as I do now,
To carve out dials quaintly, point by point,
Thereby to see the minutes how they run ;
How many make the hour full complete,
How many hours bring about the day,
How many days will finish up the year,
How many years a mortal man may live.
When this is known, then to divide the times ,
So many hours must I tend my flock,
So many hours must I take my rest,
So many hours must I contemplate,
So many hours must I sport myself ;
So many days my ewes have been with young,
So many weeks ere the poor fools will yean,
So many months ere I shall shear the fleece :
So many minutes, hours, weeks, months, and years
Past over to the end they were created,
Would bring grey hairs unto a quiet grave.
William Shakespeare.

WELL then; I now do plainly see,
   This busy world and I shall ne'er agree;
The very honey of all earthly joy
   Does of all meats the soonest cloy,
   And they, methinks, deserve my pity,
Who for it can endure the stings,
The crowd, and buzz, and murmurings
   Of this great hive, the city.

Ah, yet, ere I descend to th' grave
May I a small house and large garden have!
And a few friends, and many books, both true
   Both wise, and both delightful too!
   And since love ne'er will from me flee,
A mistress moderately fair,
And good as guardian-angels are,
   Only belov'd, and loving me!

O fountains, when in you shall I
Myself, eased of unpeaceful thoughts, espy?
O fields! O woods! when, when shall I be made
   The happy tenant of your shade?
   Here's the spring-head of pleasure's flood;
Where all the riches lie, that she
   Has coin'd and stamp'd for good.

Pride and ambition here,
Only in far-fetched metaphors appear;
Here nought but winds can hurtful murmurs scatter,
   And nought but echo flatter.

The gods, when they descended, hither
From heav'n did always choose their way
And therefore we may boldly say,
    That 'tis the way too thither.

    How happy here should I,
And one dear she live, and embracing die !
She who is all the world, and can exclude
    In deserts solitude.
    I should have then this only fear,
Lest men, when they my pleasure see,
Should hither throng to live like me,
    And make a city here.
                Abraham Cowley.

Give Me the Old ✑ ✑ ✑ ✑ ✑

Old wine to drink, old wood to burn, old books to read, and old friends to converse with.

I

OLD wine to drink !—
    Ay, give the slippery juice,
That drippeth from the grape thrown loose,
    Within the tun ;
Pluck'd from beneath the cliff
Of sunny-sided Teneriffe
And ripened 'neath the blink
    Of India's sun !

Peat whisky hot
Tempered with well-boiled water !
These make the long nights shorter—
　　Forgetting not
Good stout old English porter.

II

Old wood to burn !—
Ay, bring the hill-side beech
From where the owlets meet and screech,
　　And ravens croak ;
The crackling pine, and cedar sweet ;
Bring too, a clump of fragrant peat,
　　Dug 'neath the fern ;
　　The knotted oak,
　　A faggot too, perhaps,
Whose bright flame, dancing, winking,
Shall light us at our drinking ;
　　While the oozing sap
Shall make sweet music to our thinking.

III

Old books to read !—
Ay, bring those nodes of wit
The brazen-clasped, the vellum writ,
　　Time-honoured tomes !
The same my sire scanned before
The same my grandsire thumbèd o er
The same his sire homeward bore,
　　The well-earned meed

Of Oxford's domes.
Old Homer blind,
Old Horace, rake Anacreon, by
Old Tully, Plautus, Terence lie;
Mort Arthur's olden minstrelsie,
Quaint Burton, quainter Spenser, ay,
And Gervase Markham's venerie—
Nor leave behind
The Holy Book by which we live and die.

IV

Old friends to talk !—
Ay, bring those chosen few,
The wise, the courtly, and the true
So rarely found;
Him for my wine, him for my stud,
Him for my easel, distich, bud,
In mountain walk ! [1]

Robert H. Messinger

A Thanksgiving to God ✎ ✎ ✎

LORD, thou hast given me a cell
Wherein to dwell;
A little house, whose humble roof
Is weather proof;
Under the spars of which I lie
Both soft and dry;

[1] Two lines omitted.

Where thou, my chamber for to ward,
　　　Hast set a guard
Of harmless thoughts, to watch and keep
　　　Me, while I sleep.
Low is my porch, as is my fate ;
　　　Both void of state ;
And yet the threshold of my door
　　　Is worn by th' poor,
Who thither come, and freely get
　　　Good words, or meat.
Like as my parlour, so my hall
　　　And kitchen's small ;
A little buttery, and therein
　　　A little bin,
Which keeps my little loaf of bread
　　　Unchipt, unflead ;
Some brittle sticks of thorn or briar
　　　Make me a fire,
Close by whose living coal I sit,
　　　And glow like it.
Lord, I confess too, when I dine,
　　　The pulse is thine,
And all those other bits that be
　　　There placed by thee ;
The worts, the purslain, and the mess
　　　Of water-cress,
Which of thy kindness thou hast sent ;
　　　And my content
Makes those, and my belovèd beet,
　　　To be more sweet.

'Tis thou that crown'st my glittering hearth
  With guiltless mirth,
And giv'st me wassail bowls to drink,
  Spiced to the brink.
Lord, 'tis thy plenty-dropping hand
  That soils my land,
And giv'st me, for my bushel sown,
  Twice ten for one ;
Thou mak'st my teeming hen to lay
  Her egg each day ;
Besides, my healthful ewes to bear
  Me twins each year ;
The while the conduits of my kine
  Run cream, for wine :
All these, and better, thou dost send
  Me, to this end,—
That I should render, for my part,
  A thankful heart ;
Which, fired with incense, I resign,
  As wholly thine ;
—But the acceptance, that must be,
  My Christ, by Thee.

        Robert Herrick.

The Dirge in "Cymbeline"

FEAR no more the heat o' the sun
  Nor the furious winter's rages ;
Thou thy worldly task hast done,
  Home art gone and ta'en thy wages :

Golden lads and girls all must,
As chimney-sweepers, come to dust.

Fear no more the frown o' the great :
   Thou art past the tyrant's stroke ;
Care no more to clothe and eat ;
   To thee the reed is as the oak :
The sceptre, learning, physic, must
All follow this, and come to dust.

Fear no more the lightning-flash,
   Nor the all-dreaded thunder-stone,
Fear not slander, censure rash ;
   Thou hast finished joy and moan :
All lovers young, all lovers must
Consign to thee, and come to dust.

No exorciser harm thee !
Nor no witchcraft charm thee !
Ghost unlaid forbear thee !
Nothing ill come near thee !
   Quiet consummation have ;
   And renowned be thy grave !

William Shakespeare.

THE RETURN

The Glamour of the Town ∽   ∽   ∽

LET them talk of lakes and mountains and romantic dales—all that fantastic stuff; give me a ramble by night, in the winter nights in London —the Lamps lit—the pavements of the motley Strand crowded with to and fro passengers—the shops all brilliant, and stuffed with obliging customers and obliged tradesmen—give me the old bookstalls of London — a walk in the bright Piazzas of Covent Garden. I defy a man to be dull in such places— perfect Mahometan paradises upon earth! I have lent out my heart with usury to such scenes from my childhood up, and have cried with fullness of joy at the multitudinous scenes of Life in the crowded streets of ever dear London. . . . I don't know if you quite comprehend my low Urban Taste; but depend upon it that a man of any feeling will have given his heart and his love in childhood and in boy- hood to any scenes where he has been bred, as well to dirty streets (and smoky walls as they are called) as to green lanes, " where live nibbling sheep," and to the everlasting hills and the Lakes and ocean. A mob of men is better than a flock of sheep, and a crowd of happy faces jostling into the playhouse at the hour of six is a more beautiful spectacle to man than the shepherd driving his "silly" sheep to fold.

Charles Lamb to Robert Lloyd.

NOTE

THANKS are due to many authors and publishers for their kindness in permitting in this book the use of copyright poems and prose passages : to Mrs. Hinkson for two lyrics from *Poems* (Lawrence & Bullen); to Mrs. Meynell for extracts from *The Rhythm of Life, The Colour of Life, The Spirit of Place*, and *Poems* (all published by Mr. Lane), and for "The Lady of the Lambs"; to Mr. Lloyd Osbourne for quotations from R. L. Stevenson's *Songs of Travel, Travels with a Donkey*, and *The Merry Men* (Chatto & Windus); to the Rev. Canon Beeching for poems from *In a Garden* (Lane); to Mr. Hilaire Belloc for poems; to Mr. Henry Bernard for "Marie"; to Mr. Robert Bridges for two numbers from his *Shorter Poems* (Bell & Sons); to Mr. John Burroughs for a passage on the apple from *Winter Sunshine* (David Douglas); to Mr. Bliss Carman for poems from *Songs from Vagabondia* and *More Songs from Vagabondia*, two of which are from his own pen, and two from that of his collaborator, the late Richard Hovey (Elkin

Mathews), and also for "Daphne" from *The Pipes of Pan* (Murray); to Mr. Bertram Dobell for two songs from the selection of James Thomson's poems made and published by him; to Mr. Austin Dobson for poems from *Old World Idylls* and *At the Sign of the Lyre* (both published by Messrs. Kegan Paul & Co.); to Mr. Gerald Gould for three poems; to Mrs. W. E. Henley for two of Mr. Henley's poems from *A Book of Verses* (Nutt); to Messrs. Houghton, Mifflin & Co. for two of Whittier's poems; to Mr. Maurice Hewlett for good sentiments from *Pan and the Young Shepherd* (Lane); to Mr. Rudyard Kipling for "Sussex" from *The Five Nations* (Methuen); to Mr. R. C. Lehmann for a poem from *Crumbs of Pity* (Blackwood); to Messrs. Longmans for a passage from Richard Jefferies' *Story of my Heart*; and to the same publishers and the Executors of Mr. William Morris for two extracts from *Poems by the Way*; to Mr. J. W. Mackail for translations from his *Greek Anthology* (Longmans); to Mr. John Masefield for a poem from *Ballads* (Mathews); to Messrs. Macmillan for lyrics from the late T. E. Brown's *Poems* and Miss Rossetti's *Poems* and a passage from FitzGerald's *Letters*; to E. Nesbit for two poems from *A Pomander of Verse* (Lane) and *The Rainbow and the Rose* (Longmans); to Mr. Alfred Noyes for "Sherwood"; to Moira O'Neill for poems from her *Songs of the Glens of Antrim* (Blackwood); to Mr. Walter Ramal for a poem from his *Songs of Childhood* (Longmans); to Mr. William Sharp for a

363

quotation from Philip Bourke Marston's *Song Tide* (Scott); to Messrs. Small, Maynard & Co., and to Mr. Horace L. Traubel, one of Walt Whitman's literary executors, for extracts from *Leaves of Grass*; to the Misses Smith for a song by the late Ada Smith; to Mr. Francis Thompson for "A May Burden" from his *New Poems* (Constable); to Mr. William Watson for two songs from his *Collected Poems* (Lane); to Mr. W. B. Yeats for lyrics from his *Poems* (Fisher Unwin) and *The Wind among the Reeds* (Elkin Mathews); to Miss Cicely Fox Smith for "Afoot"; and to the Editor of the *Spectator* for allowing me to use several poems that first appeared in his pages.

From the present edition (1905) it has been necessary, owing to reasons into which I need not here enter, to omit five or six pieces that I should have wished to retain. I am very sorry to have been forced to this course, which was, I can assure the reader, no affair of mine. I have, however, added many new pieces, which will, I hope, be considered as compensation.

E. V. L.

September 1905.

UP-HILL

Does the road wind up-hill all the way?
   Yes, to the very end.
Will the day's journey take the whole long day?
   From morn to night, my friend.

But is there for the night a resting place?
   A roof for when the slow dark hours begin.
May not the darkness hide it from my face?
   You cannot miss that inn.

Shall I meet other wayfarers at night?
   Those who have gone before.
Then must I knock, or call when just in sight?
   They will not keep you standing at the door.

Shall I find comfort, travel-sore and weak?
   Of labour you shall find the sum.
Will there be beds for me and all who seek?
   Yes. beds for all who come.

Christina G. Rossetti

Printed by
MORRISON & GIBB LIMITED
Edinburgh